ANASTASIA DUKOVA

QUEENSLAND POLICE IN THE GREAT WAR

A COMPENDIUM

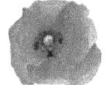

Copyright © 2024 by Anastasia Dukova

The moral rights of the author have been asserted.

ISBN 978-1-7637647-0-5

ISBN 978-1-7637647-1-2 (eBook)

This work is subject to copyright. No part of this publication may be reproduced, distributed, or transmitted in any form or by any means, including photocopying, recording, or other electronic or mechanical methods, without the prior written permission of the author, except as permitted under the *Copyright Act*.

Illustrations by Anastasia Dukova

First edition 2024

Dr Anastasia Dukova holds PhD in crime and policing history from the University of Dublin, Trinity College. She is a member of the Irish Association of Professional Historians and a Fellow of the Royal Historical Society UK. She previously held fellowships with Griffith University, State Library Queensland and the University of Toronto.

Contents

1. Acknowledgments — 1
2. Introduction — 3
3. 1914 — 21
4. 1915 — 55
5. 1916 — 105
6. 1917 — 129
7. 1918 — 135
8. Appendix A — 139

Acknowledgments

I would like to especially acknowledge research carried out by the Queensland Police Museum, its Curator Lisa Jones, Duncan Leak, Museum Assistant, and Tim Lycett, a former Victorian police officer and an experienced military genealogist. Their valuable time and resources were a critical contribution that allowed this project to come to fruition.

The Queensland Police in the Great War began as an award-winning project supported by the *Q ANZAC 100: Memories for a New Generation*, State Library of Queensland. Additional funding generously provided by the Friends of Queensland Police Museum helped the project grow to be published as a book.

Introduction

Queensland Police in the Great War: A Compendium is a biographical reference guide of the Queensland Police Force (QPF) personnel who enlisted with the Australian Imperial Forces (AIF), also known as the Anzacs (Australian and New Zealand Army Corps). Nationally, nearly half of all eligible men, or 416,809, between the ages of 18-44 volunteered. Meticulous research carried out with the assistance of the Queensland Police Museum identified and verified 174 names. This compendium is a comprehensive reference source featuring short biographies of Queensland police personnel who enlisted to fight in the First World War between 1914 and 1918. It also contains a selection of in-depth life and family stories of these men. Many of them returned from the front and resumed their duties with the Queensland Police; they went on to have long careers, in some cases their children carrying on their policing legacy.

Methodology

There were 174 names identified and verified through careful cross-referencing of *Register of Members of the Police Force* (QPF Register), 1856-1917 and 1879-1924, QPF personnel files with the series No B2455, Australian Imperial Force files held at the National Archives Australia (NAA). All recruits for the 1910s from the Queensland Police database were considered with men who resigned or were dismissed before the war began in July 1914 removed, as well as the men that were sworn in after November 1918. The remaining dataset of just under 600 names was matched with the Australian Imperial Forces files along with the Queensland Police Museum database, in conjunction with the personnel files held at the Queensland State Archives (AF series). A further targeted search of all police recruits sworn in between 1899 and 1900 identified additional 130 names, which were also matched against the sample already extracted. This selection in combination with cross-referencing yielded 200 names. In cases where there were few men with identical or similar names, biographical details such as place or date of birth helped refine the sample, finally narrowing it to 174 names.

The review of the service details of the final dataset of 174 names showed most of the men who volunteered with the AIF joined the police between 1912 and 1914, peaking in 1914. In that year nearly half of men who joined the police left either the same year or within a year to enlist. This means that some policemen only served for a few months, as the war broke out at the end of July 1914. In October 1915, Commissioner Cahill issued a Memorandum, suspending leave for enlistments due to personnel shortages. As a result, many men chose to resign from police to enlist anyway, often without declaring their intent. A few more were dismissed with a small number indicating their plans to join the war effort. In such cases, men would enlist within a few weeks of separating from police service. Recognising this fact, during the selection stage, a window of six months has been applied to the date of separation from the QPF to enlistment into the AIF.

This approach revealed men like George McRitchie, Herbert Forrest, Edward Walsh and Alex Watson, who were killed in action (KIA) but are not memorialised in the Queensland Police Honour Roll with 30 policemen who were granted war leave (their stories are also featured in Paul Ruge's *Their Glory Shall Not be Blotted Out*). This is because these men were not considered policemen as they had resigned or been dismissed before enlisting.

Of the 174 men identified with 44 enlisted in 1914; 75 in 1915; 38, including Billy Elsdale, in 1916; 12 in 1917; five in 1918. The department published internal lists of men who were granted leave or resigned to enlist with the AIF in 1916, 1920 and 1922, which contain some names that could not be matched with the NAA B2455 series, at the time of review. These are attached in the appendix. One name, Wallace O. McGillivray, does not appear in the NAA WW1 series, however, it was still included in the compendium using the self-reported information contained in the QP staff file. This is because McGillivray's name appears on the List of Officers, who have Served in the British Expeditionary Forces, or Australian Imperial Forces, and all the remaining names on the list have been confirmed to have enlisted (see Appendix A).

OFFICE OF COMMISSIONER OF POLICE,
Brisbane, 12th October, 1916.

Ref.No.1368 M.

Circular Memorandum,
No. 918.

Inspector_____

Officers in charge of Districts are advised that, owing to the depletion of the Police Force caused by a large number of members joining the Expeditionary Forces, I have decided to withhold permission for any more men to join such Forces, and applications in that behalf should not, until further orders, be forwarded to me.

[signature]

Commissioner.

Circular Memorandum No 918, Queensland Police Museum.

The book is structured chronologically with the names of men enlisted presented in alphabetical order for each of the war years, 1914 to 1918. Select sections feature longer biographies: Thomas Vincent Brennan, Patrick Joseph Moynihan, and William Harold Kenny in 1914; Arthur Albert Bock, Patrick Devine, Walter William Dumbrell, Thomas McGillycuddy and James Kissane in 1915; and Billy Elsdale in 1916. Where available, photographic references are included in the biographies. These are generally either part of the John Oxley Collection, State Library Queensland, or Queensland Police Museum (PM). There are several entries that are missing precise dates of death, parents' names, and burial sites. As more sources become accessible, these will be reviewed and updated. Not all men made it to the front due to worsening of a chronic condition or illness on the journey; most men enlisted in 1918 did not leave the country as Armistice was signed shortly after they joined up.

Private Billy Elsdale's life and service are highlighted in 1916. He is the only First Nations Australian identified across both police and military records. Distinct from the rest of the personnel in this compendium, Billy Elsdale was not a sworn police officer, but a tracker, as he was precluded from joining with full police power. Elsdale's father was of Anglo-Irish ancestry, which made Billy 'a half-caste'. In 1901, the Australian Constitution declared all Australians, including Indigenous people, to be British subjects. Despite this overarching status, in practice the rights afforded to First Nations peoples were negotiated through legislative arrangements between various states and the Commonwealth (Siobhan McDonell & Mick Dodson, 'Race, Citizenship and Military Service', in Joan Beaumont and Alison Cadzow, *Serving Our Country: Indigenous Australians, War, Defence, and Citizenship*, 2018, p. 35). The colonial (and later state) governments adopted numerous and conflicting definitions of 'Aboriginality', sometimes excluding 'half-caste' people from specific provisions and at other times including them. Blood-quantum distinction - an individual's racial category - was viewed as being based on their genealogy, so a 'half-caste' Aboriginal person was also categorised as European. In May 1917, under the pressures of the war, the military regulations were altered to allow the enlistment of 'half-castes' provided that 'one of the parents is white and of European origin'. Before 1917, it was left to the medical officer to decide on the suitability of the candidate (McDonell & Dodson, 2018, p. 41).

The Australian Research Council-funded linkage grant *Serving our Country: a history of Aboriginal and Torres Strait Islander people in the defence of Australia* documented the historical contributions of Aboriginal and Torres Strait Islander people in the Australian defence and auxiliary services from the Boer War to 2000 (Australian National University, 2014-2017), published its findings in *Serving Our Country: Indigenous Australians, War, Defence, and Citizenship*. In this contribution, John Maynard explores why First Nations men enlist: 'Were these Indigenous soldiers fighting for 'their country', for Australia or for the British Empire? He concludes that 'we cannot know the answer to this question with any certainty, since few of those who served left any record of their motivation for so doing' (Maynard, 2018, p. 66). A widely discussed motivator for enlistment was regular wages (or higher wages in some cases, which will be discussed further). However, Billy's record shows he was employed before enlisting. Maynard's conclusion echoes Billy's experience and challenges the idea that the prospect of a wage was the major motivation behind their volunteering; 'Aboriginal men did not go to war simply because they lacked options or choice' (Maynard, 2018, p. 66). In 2021, revising her *Aboriginal and Torres Strait Islander Volunteers in the AIF*, first published in 2011, authors Philippa Scarlett and Christine Cramer concluded that '[t]heir service is symbolic of the fact that Aboriginal people belonged to Australia prior to invasion and that it is their country and they are entitled to fight for it and did so (Philippa Scarlett and Christine Cramer, 'Aboriginal Service in World War One: 63 More AIF Volunteer', *Indigenous Histories*, 22 Apr 2021).

Wages could not have been a factor in Billy's case, but these should not be discounted as a motivator entirely. Besides patriotism, enlistment rates were likely initially buoyed by the base military wages, with the bulk volunteering in 1915 (*Report of the Commissioner of Police for 1916*, p. 448). The military wages were higher than an average workman's pay, and the police department paid premiums on policies (up to £1000) of insurance, as well as making contributions to the Police Superannuation Fund. Members of good character returning after the War were re-admitted to the police force. Police pay, as shown in the Police Superannuation Fund contributions for 1916, stood at 8 shillings and 6 pence per diem on a constable's rate (Police Superannuation Fund, Contributions due by Members of the Force absent with the Expeditionary Forces, 1916. Reference No 1268. M.7, QPM).

Public opinion of Australia's First World War participation and the ANZAC myth continues to evolve, which is reflected within the Australian scholarship. For most of the previous century, Australian historical works positioned the First World War as the key historical event that united the nation, with the exception of *Loyalty and Disloyalty: Social Conflict on the Queensland Homefront, 1914-18* (Allen & Unwin, 1987) by Raymond Evans. More recent scholarship discusses a nation broken by the war, explored within the seminal works by Joan Beaumont (*Broken*

Nation: Australians in the Great War, 2013); Joy Damousi (*The Conscription Conflict and the Great War* with Robin Archer, Murray Groot and Sean Scalmer, 2016; *Living with the Aftermath: Trauma, Nostalgia and Grief in Post-War Australia, 2001; Gender and War: Australians at War in the Twentieth Century, 1998*); Melanie Oppenheimer ('Shaping the Legend: The Role of the Australian Red Cross and Anzac', *Labour History*, 106, May 2014); J Brown (*Anzac's Long Shadow: The Cost of our National Obsession*, 2014); and Carolyn Holbrook (*Anzac: The Unauthorised Biography*, 2014). Michael JK Walsh and Andrekos Varnava's edited collection, *Australia and the Great War*, also offers a fresh perspective on the subject, pursuing 'Australianness, and Memory and Mythology, which when taken together examine the war as anticipated, experienced and remembered, using comparative and/ or trans-disciplinary intersecting narratives' (Michael JK Walsh and Andrekos Varnava, *Australia and the Great War*, 2014). Romain Fathi offers a different viewpoint of the evolving Australian Anzac narrative and focuses on the Villers-Bretonneux Memorial (Picardie, France), where several policemen's graves are located (see also Bart Ziino, *A Distant Grief: Australians, War Graves and the Great War*, 2007). In *Our Corner of the Somme: Australia at Villers-Bretonneux* (2019), he discusses the memorialisation of Australia's role on the Western Front and the Anzac mythology that so heavily contributes to Australians' understanding of themselves and too challenges accepted historiography.

Robert Bollard's *In the Shadow of Gallipoli* (2013) picks up where Evans left off; arguing that the First World War divided Australian society along class, ethnic and ideological lines, rather than uniting the nation by the forces of nationalism or imperialism, the necessity of sacrifice or the will for victory. Bollard argues that 'at the time of the war's declaration it was clearly understood as a war for "our" British Empire' (Bollard, p. 13). The embarkation rolls and service files show half of the volunteers identified as British nationals. His work examines events on the home front and places them within an international context, with a specific focus on the wartime strike wave, including the Great Strike of 1917, and the impact of international political events, such as the 1916 Easter Rising in Dublin.

The challenges faced by Australian police forces due to personnel shortages and operational changes imposed by the wartime are examined in major studies by G.M. O'Brien (*The Australian Police Forces,* 1960), Ross Johnston (*The Long Blue Line: A History of Queensland Police,* 1992), Robert Haldane (*The People's Force: A History of Victoria Police,* 1986), Robert Clyne (*Colonial Blue: A History of the South Australian Police Force, 1836-1916,* 1987) and Mark Finnane (*Policing in Australia Historical Perspectives,* 1987; *Police and Government, Histories of Policing in Australia,* 1994; "Police Rules and the Organisation of Policing in Queensland, 1905-1916", *The Australian and New Zealand Journal of Criminology, Vol. 22, No 2,* 1989). Finnane places police within a wider scope of international labour relations and the rise of an organised working-class consciousness against the backdrop of the Great War and beyond (*When Police Unionise, the Politics of Law and Order in Australia,* Institute of Criminology, 2002). Police departments staffed largely with working-class men found themselves caught between social and governmental expectations, their roles increasingly politicised.

'The Policeman as a Political Issue'

Australian recruitment offices opened in August 1914, and by the end of the year more than 50,000 men volunteered. By the end of 1915, a further 1,650,000 men volunteered to fight. However, by the middle of 1915, enlistments had started to decline as news reports from Europe were detailing the truths and difficulties of war, and the casualties to date. In 1916, the AIF was struggling to maintain the full strength of its contingent in Europe, leading Australian Prime Minister Billy Hughes to announce on 30 August 1916 the government's intent to hold a referendum to introduce a conscription policy, in which men and women over 21 years of age were eligible to vote, excluding the First Nations peoples. Conscription became a contentions topic and the debate divided Australian society, with political and social elites voicing their support of the policy change. At the same time, 'the bitterest opponent of conscription was the labour movement' both in Australia and across the British Empire (Bollard, p. 77). In addition to the class divide, the 'yes' and 'no' supporters were split along the religious lines; the Protestants were in favour and the Roman Catholics were against the conscription (with the Irish Catholics likely further radicalised after the leaders of the 1916 Rising were executed by the British government).

The anti-conscription campaigns manifested in popular meetings and demonstrations, bolstered by the shocking casualty tolls. The influence of the labour movement made all the difference in Australia, as crowds of up to 100,000 began gathering in anti-conscription rallies such as on the eve of the second referendum in 1917. Inevitably, police were called in to control the crowds. In Sydney, Melbourne, Adelaide, Perth and Brisbane local policemen did their part to preserve life and property. This did not always go to plan and sometimes led to violence. During a regional meeting in NSW, a policeman had to draw his revolver to ensure hooliganism would not get beyond bounds. In contrast, in a Melbourne women's meeting, a few policemen were placed there to keep order became 'victims' of a protest dance, where several women 'tried to swing the constables into the dance with them' (Bollard, 85); while in Warwick, Queensland, an egg thrown from the crowd at Prime Minister Billy Hughes and an ensuing 'under-reaction' by the local police resulted in calls for establishment of the Commonwealth Police 'uncontaminated' by Sinn Fein sympathies (QPF had a high proportion of Irish-born in the ranks, see Dukova 2016 for details). Hughes openly blamed the Irish Catholics for the failure of the conscription referendum.

In the aftermath of the egg incident, Hughes singled out Senior Sergeant Kenny, brother of William Harold Kenny featured in 1914 section, and insisted on dismissal, describing his conduct as 'disgraceful, disobedient, and partisan'. The January 1918 issue of the *Queensland Police Union Journal* (QPUJ) covered the incident and the investigation, and provided the departmental perspective:

> A wire to that effect caused the Premier to have a summary investigation made with a view of ascertaining the facts of the case. The result of the inquiry showed the charges to have been gross exaggerations, and far from refusing to protect the Prime Minister or failing to convert order out of chaos, it was shown that Senior Sergeant Kenny's course of action was such that saved the Prime Minister from serious assault and prevented a more hostile demonstration from developing into a riot of disastrous consequences. It transpired that, instead of deserving dismissal, Senior Sergeant Kenny's action warranted promotion for his tact.

'The Policeman as a Political Issue', *QPUJ*, 1 Jan 1918, p. 1

The *QPUJ* was launched on 1 July 1917, as the official organ of the recently formed Queensland Police Union, greeting its readers as 'comrades and friends' ('Police! Ourselves Police!', *QPUJ*, 1 Jul 1917, p. 1). The publication set out to 'stubbornly refuse to recognise any class, creed, or politics'. The pages of the 1917 issues were taken up with the union cause, pay and promotion conditions, and to a much smaller degree, the War. The conditions of a policeman's lot were such that he 'toiled the long weary days and lonely nights on a starvation wage without demur; and ... dare not express [one's] mind in protest' for fear of being handed the sack or 'carpeted' prior to departure to the 'Siberia of Queensland', Birdsville ('Be Loyal to the Union', *QPUJ*, 1 Jul 1917, p. 2). Ordinary police pay was 10 shillings and 4 pence a day, while a labourer's wage stood at 15 shillings for a regulated eight-hour day ('Deputations to the Premier. Increases Sought for and Granted', *QPUJ*, 1 Jul 1917, p. 6).

Hansard 37

Unyielding, Hughes also accused the Queensland police of anti-conscription sentiments and disloyalty, alleging another incident where his censors were impeded by the police, in their attempt to confiscate copies of the infamous *Hansard 37* in 1917 ('Hansard Seized. Action in Queensland. Government Printing Office Raided. Prime Minister's Plain Speaking', *Sydney Morning Herald*, 28 Nov 1918, p. 11). On 22 November 1917, the Queensland Legislative Assembly debated military censorship and its impact on conscription debates. Queensland Premier Thomas J Ryan, moved that:

this House emphatically protests against the manner in which the censorship is being abused to suppress reports of the views of those opposing the Commonwealth Government's conscription proposals, and condemns it as an unwarrantable interference with the rights of free discussion on the platform, and in the Press, upon the gravest issues ever submitted to the public...

Military Censorship', *Legislative Assembly*, 22 Nov 1917, p. 3132

Ryan went on to state that he would not allow for any lies to be published on the matter, and any person who does should be 'dealt with' under ordinary law, such as the Defamation Act. Parliamentary records are subject to public distribution, however, the Military Censor did not deem the object of the debates fit for public circulation and denied their transmission.

According to the *Queensland Government Gazette (QGG): Extraordinary* issue No 213 Volume CIX from 27 November 1917, a memorandum from the Military Censor, Captain JJ Stable, 1st Military District, forbade the printer and publisher of *Parliamentary Debates of the Legislative Council and the Legislative Assembly of Queensland*, 'to print or publish in contravention of the *War Precautions Regulations 1915*, any matter being or purporting to be a report of a debate in the Legislative Assembly on the 22nd day of November, 1917 (also known as *'Hansard 37'*), on the question of Military Censorship' (JJ Stables, Captain, 'Commonwealth Military Forces, 1st Military District' No. S.B. 7706 from 23 Nov 1917', *QGG: Extraordinary*, Vol CIX, No 213, QSA ID 2119770, p. 272). In his response, Cumming, the printer, expressed his 'complete surprise' at the directive and indicated that the Official Report of the debates referred in the Memorandum had been printed and published before said Memorandum was received. He went on to suggest that the proper course in the circumstances would be 'to apply immediately to the proper Court for an injunction to restrain further publication of the Report complained of, and so to test the validity of the claim set out in [the] Memorandum' (AJ Cumming, 'Proposed Censorship of "Hansard"', 24 Nov 1917, *QGG: Extraordinary*, Vol CIX, No 213. QSA ID 2119770, p. 1716). Instead, late at night on 26 November, the military authorities raided the Queensland Government Printing Office and seized thousands of copies of *Hansard 37*. The following day, Ryan stated in clear terms that per *Commonwealth Parliamentary Debates 1914-15-16*, 'the Censor had no power to censor the official report of Parliamentary Debates of any of the States', and that the censorship of the speeches was under the control of the Speaker exclusively (TJ Ryan, Premier, 'Urgent' from 27 Nov 1917, *QGG: Extraordinary*, Vol CIX, No 213. QSA Item ID 2119770, pp. 1716-17). He went on to express protest against 'such an invasion of the rights of a sovereign State' and request that Hughes, as a Prime Minister of the Commonwealth 'at once give instructions to the Postal Authorities in Queensland to transmit those copies of Queensland "Hansard" No. 37 in their possession' (QSA ID 2119770, p. 1716).

Ryan made it plain that his 'Government will take the necessary steps with the legal means at its disposal to inform the public on the matter', and in the meantime, he expressed 'the hope that all citizens will respect the law and maintain the strictest order' (QSA ID 2119770, p. 1717). Following the raid, from 2pm on 27 November to 11.15am on 29 November 1917, two non-commissioned officers (NCOs) and five to six constables were posted on round the clock duty at the Government Printing Office ('Relative to the Police on duty at the Government Printing Office, Time, and Names of the Men on Each Relief, Brisbane District, Roma Street',

3 Dec 1917, *Police Department. Police Service Commissioner's Office*. QSA ID 2039073). At about 12.30am on 28 Nov 1917, Captain Stephens from the Military Authorities along with 11 men assembled at the back gate leading to the Government Printing Office, William Street (QSA ID 2039073; QSA ID 21253557). Having identified himself, Captain Stephens demanded to go into the Office. Acting Sergeant Thomas (Reg No 135) responded that he could not let him in. The Printer, Cumming, then opened the gate and let the man in. 'After about ten minutes they both came back and Captain Stephens went away. After the Captain left, Mr Cumming said that he did not go through the Office; that he took his word that everything was alright' ('A Letter to the Sub Inspector of Police, City from Acting Sergeant Thomas Claire', QSA ID 21253557). There is no evidence to indicate the Queensland Police Force took upon themselves to arbitrarily 'bar' the censors from entering the Government Printer's premises. The exchange that took place hardly reflects the degree of hostility and anti-government sentiment depicted by the Prime Minister. That said, the Premier was very well-regarded within the Queensland Police Force, having proven himself 'a policeman's premier'. Thomas J Ryan 'was born to Irish immigrant parents during their voyage to Australia in 1852' (E Malcolm & D Hall, *A New History of the Irish in Australia*, 2018, p. 296). He was a shearer, a unionist and a Catholic. On 1 November 1917, the *Queensland Police Union Journal* (*QPUJ*) issue, eulogised Ryan:

> The display of statesmanship which shines through the gloom and chaos of a world war, together with the recent industrial upheaval in Australia, stands to the everlasting credit of Mr Ryan. At present time he looms out as a giant among the Premiers of the various parts of Commonwealth,

and on every occasion that he crossed swords with an opponent, however, powerful, Ryan always scored a palpable hit. The greatest good for the greatest number: is what Mr Ryan achieved in Queensland. His whole career as Premier stands out boldly as a new departure from the conventional rules set out by his predecessors. His fame as a legal luminary has spread far and wide. He has won every great case that he tackled, although always fighting against great odds.

'Hon TJ Ryan. Premier, Chief Secretary, and Attorney-General,' *QPUJ*, 1 Nov 1917, p. 7.

In June 1917, or approximately four months before the printer's raid, the Police Union submitted a deputation to the Premier, asking for a pay rise and changes to the superannuation scheme. It was argued that 'a Policeman had to deal with the very worst class of people was always on duty, and he had to meet the murderer, the thief, and the lunatic, and all classes of undesirables', while working unregulated hours ('Deputation to the Premier. Increases Sought for and Granted', *QPUJ*, 1 Jul 1917, p. 5). The pay rise was granted.

Following the November Government Printers raid the reporting tone changed. The first issue of *QPUJ* in 1918, opened with an editorial showcasing dismay at the politicisation of a policeman: 'political opportunists came and went', according to the editorial titled 'The Policeman as a Political Issue', 'but the ancient and worthy force of the King's Constabulary was not considered to be profitable capital to be exploited by men and parties wanting political control.' (The Policeman as a Political Issue', *QPUJ*, 1 Jan 1918, p. 1). The editorial suggested the police carried out their orders to protect State property, following the extraordinary order of

Prime Minister to ransack the State Government Printing Office all while threatening the Premier and Cabinet Ministers. The bitter response by the Prime Minister, according to the *QPUJ*, was caused by Hughes' 'powerlessness to carry out further predatory work that no doubt has been contemplated' (*QPUJ*, 1 Jan 1918, p. 1). Hughes' retaliation was considered an attempt to exploit the Queensland Police Force for the 'purpose of making capital for vote snatching politicians' (*QPUJ*, 1 Jan 1918, p. 2). Despite the politicisation of the police department, the enlistment numbers for the Queensland policemen followed the general population trend, ramping up throughout 1914 and into 1915 (leave ban, notwithstanding), and tapering off in 1916 and 1917. Having said that, although the department was distancing itself from federal politics, it became more entangled with the state government.

Further reading

Brannigan, Niall and John Kirwan. *Kilkenny Families in the Great War*, 2012.

Dukova, Anastasia. *A History of the Dublin Police and its Colonial Legacy*. Palgrave Macmillan, 2016.

Ruge, Paul. *Their Glory Shall Not be Blotted Out: 30 Queensland Police Officers Who Died on Active Service During the Great War 1914-18*.

Scarlett, Philippa and Christine Cramer. 'Aboriginal Service in World War One: 63 More AIF Volunteer', *Indigenous Histories*, 22 Apr 2021.

1914

Samuel Alexander ANDERSON (22 May 1886 - 25 Aug 1956), described as 5' 10" tall, fresh complexion with blue eyes and brown hair, Presbyterian (*QPF Recruit Register*). Born to George and Margaret in Strabane, County Tyrone, Ireland. Sworn into the QPF on 3 Mar 1914, 27yrs 9mths, Reg no 1823, Stables, Petrie Terrace Police Depot, Brisbane (QSA AF3379). Given leave to re-join the Imperial Forces and reported for duty 3 Oct 1914 SERN 6413 with 8 Huss. Embarked from Melbourne aboard HMAT *Miltiades A28* on 21 Oct 1914. Served eight years with the 8th (King's Royal Irish) Hussars. Resumed duty with the QPF on 18 Sep 1919, 33yrs 6mths, Reg No 1823, Stables, Petrie Terrace Police Depot, Brisbane. Resigned 10 Feb 1921 (QSA AF3379). Died 25 Aug 1956 and buried in Brisbane.

Gilbert McClymont BECK (17 Sep 1886 - 25 Apr 1939), described as 5' 8 ¾" tall, fair complexion, blue eyes and dark brown hair, Presbyterian (*QPF Recruit Register*). Born to Hugh and Margaret in Kilkeel, County Down, Ireland (*Census, 1901* Ireland). Sworn into the QPF on 11 Jul 1912, 25yrs 10mths, Reg no 1627, Roma Street Station (QSA AF4490). Called to serve as a reservist with the Royal Field Artillery on 13 Aug 1914, Reg No 34683. Returned to Australia in 1919. Married Mary Jane Hassard on 16 Apr 1919. Resumed duty with the QPF on 4 Sep 1919, 32yrs, Roma Street Station (QSA AF4490). Died 25 Apr 1939, buried in plot 28-45-2 at the Toowong Cemetery, Brisbane. Honours: Queensland Police Medal for Merit (1913); 1914/1915 Star; 1919 British War Medal; 1919 Victory Medal.

Henry BELL (28 Dec 1888 – 23 Sep 1964) described as 5' 9" tall, dark complexion with brown eyes and black hair, Church of England (*QPF Recruit Register*). Born to Henry and Mary in Yengarie, Queensland (NAA 3008628). Sworn into the QPF on 5 Jun 1913, 24yrs 5mths, Reg no 1725, Roma Street Station, Brisbane. Resigned 15 May 1914 (QSA AF2887). Enlisted into the AIF SERN 284 on 9 Sep 1914. Embarked with the 9th Australian Battalion aboard HMAT *Omrah A5* on 24 Sep 1914. Received bullet wound to back and neck at Gallipoli on 12 Jun 1915, and was invalided back to London via Malta. Returned to Australia 8 Oct 1915, discharged from the AIF on 25 Jan 1916 (NAA 3008628). Died 23 Sep 1964 and buried in a Maryborough cemetery. Honours: 1914/1915 Star; British War Medal; 1919 Victory Medal.

James Alan BRADLEY (17 Jan 1895 - 12 Mar 1974), described as 5' 9" tall, ruddy complexion with hazel eyes and brown hair, Methodist (*QPF Recruit Register*). Born to William and Annabella in Kilcoy, Queensland. Sworn into the QPF on 29 Oct 1914, 19yrs 9mths, Reg no 1939, Roma Street Station, Brisbane (QSA AF3186). Enlisted SERN 468 with the AIF on 19 Nov 1914. Embarked with the 2nd Australian Light Horse Field Ambulance on 15 Dec 1914. Returned to Australia on HT *Argyllshire* on 23 December 1918. Resigned from the QPF on 27 Feb 1919 (QSA AF3186). Died 12 Mar 1974 and buried in Brisbane. Honours: 1914/1915 Star; British War Medal; 1919 Victory Medal. Photographs: PM4548; *The Queenslander Pictorial*, supplement to *The Queenslander*, 26 Dec 1914, p. 26 (SLQ Image No 702692-19141226-s0026-0047).

Thomas Vincent BRENNAN (06 Oct 1889 - 07 Sep 1920), was born in Kilkenny City, County Kilkenny, Ireland on 6 October 1889 (NAA Series B2455 Item 6512081). His mother Mary (née Byrne) Brennan was a newsagent, stationer and a boarding housekeeper in High St, opposite St James Street. John Brennan, Tom's father, was a butcher. *1901 Census Ireland* shows Mary (38), as widowed and living with Thomas's two younger brothers, Joseph (6) and Anthony (3, dob 23 Jan 1898). Tom's other siblings were John Patrick (b Flood St, KK City, 8 Jul 1886), Leo Mary (b 29 Jan 1888), Josephine 'Phina' (b 20 Mar 1891) & Helen Teresa (b 22 Jan 1893) (Brannigan & Kirwan, p. 36). The family was Roman Catholic and spoke both Irish and English at home. Tom was locally known as the Poet. He had dark complexion, hazel eyes and brown hair.

On 16 April 1908, Brennan left London for Brisbane on an immigrant ship *Orontes* arriving at his destination on 4 June 1908, as an assisted immigrant (*Assisted Immigration 1848 to 1912*, M1797/08 p. 158, QSA 18490). Brennan joined the Queensland Police Force on 29 April 1909 (QSA AF2699). He was sworn in on 31 May, aged 19 years, Reg no 1248. On 26 November 1913, Constable Brennan was transferred to the Brisbane Criminal Investigation Bureau, where he was employed as a Police Gazette clerk.

On 14 January 1914, Tom's younger brother Joseph Francis (Joe) also left home for Brisbane, arriving on the ship *Roscommon* from London in March (*UK & Ireland, Outward Passenger Lists, 1890-1960*). Joe got a job as a labourer with W.C Harding, solicitor, Inns of Court, Adelaide Street. He also had previously done a two-year apprenticeship as a butcher (Brannigan & Kirwan, p. 34). On 7 December 1914, Joe enlisted with the AIF (SERN 1312), aged 20 years and 3 months.

On 10 December 1914, Tom Brennan resigned from QPF and enlisted with the Medical Corps (SERN 565). On 13 February 1915, he and Joe embarked for Egypt together, on HMAT *Seang Choon*, bound for the Mediterranean Expeditionary Forces (MEF) (NAA Series B2455 Item 3117181). Joe Brennan was later taken on strength of the 9th Battalion. In March, Tom was taken on strength of the 2nd Light Horse Field Brigade, Ambulance. The Brigade was formed in September 1914 as part of the 2nd Contingent, attached to the Australian Division. On 15 May 1915, he embarked for Gallipoli. Brennan regularly wrote home to his parents from Anzac Cove (Brannigan & Kirwan, p. 36).

On 19 June 1915, Joe was severely wounded to the head and hand at Gaba Tepe. Just under a month later, on 14 July 1915, he died at the Egyptian Government Hospital, Alexandria. Mrs Mary (née Byrne) Brennan learned first of Joe's death in the local newspaper. On 4 September 1915, she also began receiving a fortnightly survivor's pension of £2. In October 1916, his mother angrily returned the personal effects of 'Pte John Brennan, 9th ALH, regl no 378', which had been sent to her in error. In June 1917, Tom followed up with the Army regarding his brother's lost effects and in May 1918, the Army asserted that 'every effort had been made to locate the effects', but that everything evacuated with Joe had been government property (Joseph Brennan NAA Series B2455 Item 3117056). Shortly after receiving news of his brother's death, Tom wrote a lament for all the men lost in the way. On 6 December 1915, his poem titled 'Our Nameless Dead' was widely circulated and published in *The Northern Miner*, a Charters Towers publication.

Only a month after Joseph Brennan's death, on 3 August 1915, Tom left for Alexandria via Malta, disembarking on Christmas Eve day (NAA Item 3117181). Tom's battalion marched to Serapeum, arriving two months later in February 1916. The months that followed were plagued with intermittent but regular fighting. On 22 July 1916, Brennan was appointed corporal. Shortly after he was awarded a Military Medal and received a mention in Gen A J Murray's dispatch which recounted the attacks and counterattacks over July-September in the region:

> The complete result of the operations in the Katia district [east of the Suez Canal] was the decisive defeat of an enemy force amounting in all to some 18,000, including 15,000 rifles. Some 4,000 prisoners, including 50 officers, were captured, and, from the number of enemy dead actually buried, it is estimated that the total number of enemy casualties amounted to about 9,000.

Sir Archibald Murray's Despatches, June 1916 - June 1917, J M Dent & Son Ltd., 1920, p. 72.

In July 1917, Corporal Tom Brennan was transferred to the Camel Brigade Field Ambulance in Moascar, Egypt and the following day assigned to 5th ALH Field Ambulance and promoted to Sergeant on 5 July. A fortnight later he was treated in Camel Brigade Field Ambulance, Rafa, for a groin staff [staphylococcus] infection (NAA Item 3117181).

In the meantime, in Ireland, Tom's other brother, Anthony, also joined the war, enlisting with the 2nd Battalion Royal Irish Regiment (11th Brigade, 4th Division) on 27 July 1915. He was only 17 years and 2 months. The recruiting officer assured his mother that Anthony would not be sent to the Front until after his 19th birthday. She sent a copy of his birth certificate to the Richmond Barracks, only to have it returned, saying her son had already embarked for France. The recruiting officer falsified his age on the enlistment papers and the Army subsequently refused to return him home from the Front. The *Daily Mail* covered the scandal, which involved the MP, P O'Brien, the Under Secretary for War, H J Tennant, and others (Brannigan & Kirwan, p. 30). Anthony's best friend, Francis (Frank) Waldron and Tom Tobin also enlisted. In fact, many of the town's young men did. Francis was killed in action at the Somme aged only 19 years (Brannigan & Kirwan, p. 505).

Thomas Rowe, a stretcher bearer, helped Anthony Brennan's search for his friend's Frank body at 'Bazentin following the battalion's fight on 14 July 1916, but they were both unsuccessful (Brannigan & Kirwan, p. 450). Rowe was 'regularly entrusted with men's farewell letters prior to an attack', including Pte Anthony Brennan, who wrote his 'final' letter home in Jun 1917. George Buckley was another of Anthony's friends and Kilkenny City local killed on the day (Brannigan & Kirwan, p. 45). According to *Kilkenny Families in the Great War*, many of the Brennans' friends enlisted at the time and very few returned to Ireland.

Anthony was wounded in the legs by an HE (high-explosive) shell on the evening of 3-4 August 1917. Following the shelling, he spent a year in various hospitals (Napsbury, near St Albans for five months, then D Castle Red Cross Hospital, a Convalescent Home, and then an orthopaedic hospital in Blackrock, Co Dublin). He was discharged from the military on 26 September 1918. While at the front, his mother and sister, Josephine 'Phina', and Tom, all wrote to him regularly (Brannigan & Kirwan, p. 30).

By early 1918, capitalising on his talent as an author and a writer, Tom was a joint editor and contributor to *The Cacolet*, the journal of the Australian

Field Ambulance in Palestine. He wrote under the *nome de plume* 'Brentonman'.

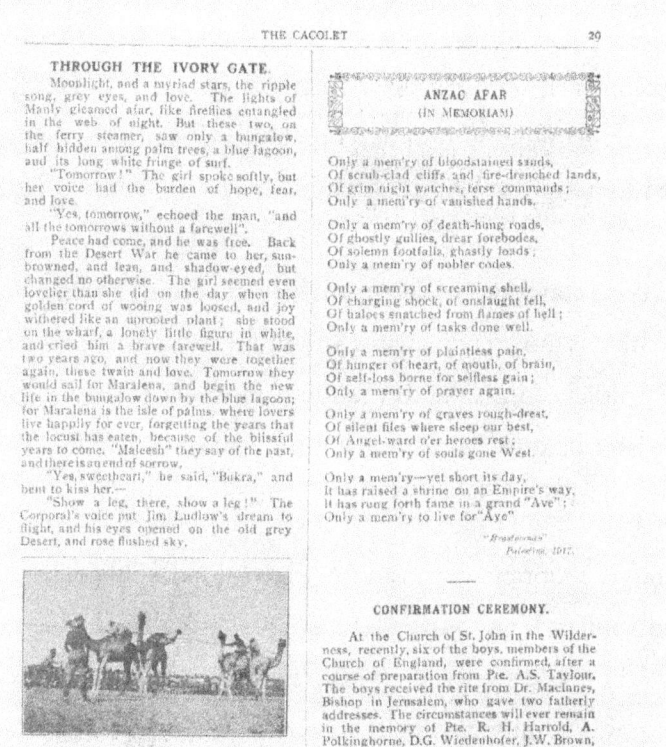

'*Anzac Afar, In Memoriam*', The Cacolet, No 3, September 1917, p. 29.

In July 1919, Brennan embarked from Port Said, Egypt, aboard HT *Tagus* for '10% leave' in the UK. In September, he became 'dangerously ill', attempted to cut his throat, and was admitted to Queen Alexandria Hospital, Millbank, London. The next month, Tom was transferred to Lord Derby War Hospital suffering from hallucinations and fits of violence (NAA Item 3117181). Having spent months fighting in the desert with causalities in the thousands, Tom was suffering from severe post-traumatic stress which was not yet recognised.

On 9 December, he embarked for Australia aboard HT *Borda*, as 'mental case'. Brennan's condition deteriorated and on during the voyage he attempted to jump overboard. Upon his arrival in Sydney on 2 February 1920, he was admitted to 27th Army Hospital. Tom was discharged on 4 April 1920 as a convalescent, free from hallucinations. The medical report described him as quiet and amiable and fit for work. Brennan returned to Brisbane, initially to Blaxlands (Soldiers' Home), Appel St, South Brisbane. He later boarded with Mrs Winnie Smith, 'Kirribilli', Tribune St, South Brisbane (NAA Series MT1486/1 Item 6512081).

On 12 May 1920, Brennan was admitted to the Staff Officer Invalided and Returned Soldiers Unit (SOI & RS), but just over a fortnight later, on 30 May 1920, he was discharged on his own request. Two months later, on 31 July, he was admitted to Brisbane General Hospital with a fractured spine, following a fall from the balcony at Westcourt (a boarding-house) in Tank street the night before (*Brisbane Courier*, 6 Jul 1920, p. 6; 2 Aug 1920, p. 4). Brennan died on 7 September 1920, with 'exhaustion' provided as the cause of death (1920/B/32846). He is buried at South Brisbane Cemetery, 2H-304. Honours: 1914/1915 Star; 1916 Mentioned in Despatches (*Comm of Aus Gazette*, 19 Apr 1917, p. 926, position 96); 1916 Military Medal (*Comm of Aus Gazette*, 19 Apr 1917, p. 924, position 19); British War Medal; 1919 Victory medal.

Thomas James Joseph CASEY (14 Mar 1889 - 07 May 1977), described as 5' 9 ½" tall, fresh complexion with grey eyes and brown hair, Roman Catholic (*QPF Recruit Register*). Born to T and H in Greenwich, Kent, England. Sworn into the QPF on 2 Sept 1913, 24yrs 5mths, Reg no 1753, Roma Street Station, Brisbane (QSA AF4894). Reported for duty on 13 August 1914. Embarked from Sydney aboard HMAT *Miltiades A28* on 17 Oct 1914. Served for seven years with the 1st Coldstream Guards at Windsor. Returned to Australia on 19 Mar 1919 (NAA Series MT1487/1 Item 6036568). Resumed police duty on 15 May 1919, 29yrs 2mths, Reg no 1753, Petrie Terrace Police Depot, Brisbane. Married Olive Brown on 4 Apr 1921. Retired 20 Feb 1946 (QSA AF4894). Died 7 May 1977 and buried in plot LAWN-2-659 in the Hemmant Cemetery, Brisbane.

Peter John CLOHERTY (17 Sep 1889 - May 1924), described as 5' 9 ¾" tall, pale complexion with blue eyes and fair hair, Roman Catholic (*QPF Recruit Register*). Born to John and Mary, Ireland. Served in the Royal Irish Constabulary, 4 Sep 1914 to 16 Jan 1914. Sworn into the QPF on 25 Mar 1914, 24yrs 6mths, Reg no 1835, Petrie Terrace Police Depot (QSA AF3200). Enlisted with the AIF SERN 964 on 3 Sep 1914. Embarked with the 9th Australian Infantry Battalion aboard HMAT *Omrah A5* on 24 Sep 1914. Married Mary Elizabeth Wear while on leave in England, St Michael at Bowes, Southgate on 8 Feb 1917. Returned to Australia via MV Berrima on 31 Oct 1917 suffering from pleurisy. Discharged medically unfit from the army on 9 Feb 1918 (Enlistment paperwork). Resigned from the QPF on 5 Mar 1918 (QSA AF3200). Died in May 1924 and buried in plot 10-33-3 at Toowong Cemetery. Honours: 1914/1915 Star; 1919 British War Medal; 1919 Victory Medal.

Phillip CONNOR (23 Nov 1881 - 13 Aug 1937), described as 6' tall, fresh complexion with blue eyes and brown hair, Roman Catholic (*QPF*

Recruit Register). Born in Shankill, Galway, Ireland. Served in the Royal Irish Constabulary, 4 May 1908 to 30 Apr 1913. Sworn into the QPF on 2 Sep 1913, 31yrs 9mths, Reg no 1754, Roma Street Station, Brisbane (QSA AF3401). Imperial Reservist recalled to the 1st Irish Guards, reported for duty 13 Aug 1914. Embarked aboard HMAT Miltiades A28 on 17 Oct 1914. Suffered a gunshot wound to the right knee in front line near Poelcapelle, Belgium and was returned to Australia on 9 Jul 1918. Re-appointed to the QPF on 24 Jul 1919, 37yrs, Bundaberg Station, Queensland. Discharged 3 May 1921. Died 13 Aug 1937 and buried in the Lutwyche Cemetery, Brisbane.

William Gerald CUMMINS (27 Feb 1892 - 4 Aug 1979), described as 5' 9 ¼" tall, fresh complexion with blue eyes and black hair, Roman Catholic (*QPF Recruit Register*). Born to James and ? in Galway, Ireland. Sworn into the QPF on 30 Sep 1913, 21yrs 7mths, Reg no 1768, Roma Street Station, Brisbane (QSA AF3500). Enlisted with the AIF SERN 1330 on 24 Dec 1914. Embarked with the 9th Australian Infantry Battalion aboard HMAT *Seang Bee A48* on 13 Feb 1915. Returned to Australia on 1 Jul 1916 (Enlistment paperwork). Resumed QPF duty 11 Jan 1917. Resigned 15 Oct 1922 (QSA AF3500). Died 4 Aug 1979 and buried in plot ANZAC-2-A-40 at Mt Gravatt Cemetery, Brisbane. Honours: 1914/1915 Star; British War Medal; 1919 Victory medal.

George DEWHURST (05 Sep 1893 - 05 Nov 1916 KIA), described as 5' 8" tall, ruddy complexion with blue eyes and brown hair, Church of England (*QPF Recruit Register*). Born to Thomas and Annie in Blackpool, Lancashire, England. Sworn into the QPF on 11 Feb 1914, Reg no 1806, Roma Street, Brisbane. Resigned. Enlisted with the AIF SERN 616 on 29 Dec 1914. Embarked with the 25th Australian Infantry Battalion aboard HMAT *Aeneas A60* on 29 Jun 1915. George survived action at Anzac

Cove in 1915 and a bout of jaundice, which took him months to recover. He re-joined his battalion in France on 30 Sept 1916, at Abelle. Just after midnight on 5 Nov 1916 at Flers, whilst with others digging a jumping off trench in preparation for an upcoming attack, Dewhurst was shot through the body by a sniper and died within minutes. His body was exhumed and identified in 1922 and re-buried in plot 24-J-8 in the Caterpillar Valley Cemetery, Longueval, Picardie, France. Honours: 1914-15 Star; British War Medal; Victory Medal. Photographs: PM0589; AWM Accession No. P01202.001; *The Queenslander Pictorial*, supplement to *The Queenslander*, 06 Feb 1915, p. 24 (SLQ Image No 702692-19150206-s0024-0010). Killed in action.

Andy Albury GILBY (10 Apr 1890 - 21 Mar 1961), described as 5' 9" tall, fair complexion with blue eyes and hair, Presbyterian (*QPF Recruit Register*). Born to George and Emma in Crookwell, Upper Lachlan Shire, New South Wales. Sworn into the QPF on 1 Sep 1914, Reg no 1912, Petrie Terrace Police Depot Stables, Brisbane (QSA AF3185). Enlisted with the AIF SERN 566 on 7 Nov 1914. Embarked with the 5th Australian Light Horse Regiment aboard HMAT *Persic A34* on 21 Dec 1914. Proceeded to Gallipoli 16 May 1915. Severely wounded in action 8 Jul 1915, and again on 10 Aug 1917. Returned to Australia on 23 Oct 1918 (Attestation Papers). Resigned from the QPF on 25 Feb 1919. Married Ethel Waples at Casino on 16 Jul 1919. Died 21 Mar 1961 and buried in Casino Cemetery, New South Wales. Honours: 1914/1915 Star; British War Medal; 1919 Victory medal.

Edmond Joseph GORMAN (14 Sep 1893 - 3 Nov 1976), described as 6' ¾" tall, ruddy complexion with blue eyes and brown hair, Roman Catholic (*QPF Recruit Register*). Born to Patrick and Bridget in Yarrawonga, Victoria. Sworn into the QPF on 1 Aug 1914, 22yrs, Reg no 1886, Petrie Terrace

Police Depot Stables, Brisbane. Enlisted with the AIF SERN 712 on 1 Sept 1914. Embarked with the 9th Australian Infantry Battalion in 1914. Served one year and 43 days active service in Egypt and Gallipoli, returned home medically unfit. Resigned from the QPF 5 Feb 1917 (QSA AF5953). Re-enlisted with the AIF SERN 712A on 29 Mar 1917. Embarked with the 11th Australian Machine Gun Company aboard HMAT *Nestor A71* on 21 Nov 1917. Returned to Australia on 28 Feb 1919 (Attestation papers). Re-appointed to the QPF on 27 Jan 1920, 28yrs, Reg no 2434, South Brisbane station. Married Agnes Ellen Comerford on 2 Dec 1924 at Longreach, Queensland. Retired on 14 Sep 1953 (QSA AF5953). Died 3 Nov 1976 and buried in plot A-12-27 in Belgian Gardens Cemetery, Townsville. Honours: 1914/1915 Star; British War Medal; 1919 Victory medal. Photograph: PM4552.

John Clare GRAHAM (1 Feb 1892 - 22 Sep 1917 KIA), described as 5' 10 ¾" tall, ruddy complexion with hazel eyes and fair hair, Roman Catholic (*QPF Recruit Register*). Born to Bernard and Maria in Toowoomba, Queensland. Sworn into the QPF on 2 Sep 1913, 21yrs 7mths, Reg no 1758, Roma Street Station (QSA AF3030). Enlisted in the AIF on 9 Oct 1914 SERN 1136. Embarked with the 1st Australian Infantry Battalion aboard HMAT *Themistocles A32* on 22 Dec 1914. Received shrapnel wounds in his back while fighting in Belgium and succumbed to these wounds on 22 Sep 1917. Graham was the only Queensland Police officer to have fought on all three fronts - Gallipoli, France and Belgium. Buried in plot 24-C-18 of the Lijssenthock Military Cemetery, Belgium. Honours: 1914/1915 Star; 1916 Distinguished Conduct Medal; British War Medal; 1919 Victory medal. Photographs: PM0111 (QPM Collection). Killed in action.

Henry HACKNEY (7 Oct 1880 - 1951), described as 5' 8" tall, fresh complexion with blue eyes and brown hair, Church of England (*QPF Recruit Register*). Born to Thomas and Ann in Appleton, Widnes, Lancashire, England. Sworn into the QPF on 23 May 1910, 27yrs 7mths, Reg no 1332, Roma Street, Brisbane (QSA AF3388). Enlisted with the AIF SERN 59 on 28 Aug 1914. Embarked with the 2nd Australian Light Horse Regiment aboard HMAT *Star of England A15* on 24 Sep 1914. Served with the 19th Hussars for seven years, 5 years in Reserves and the Lancashire Volunteers engineers for two years (Attestation Papers). Married Ivy Lillian Whitbread in 1917 while on leave. Captain Hackney returned to Australia on 7 Sep 1919. Resigned from the QPF on 1 Apr 1921 (QSA AF3388). Went onto serve in WW2. Honours: 1 Jan 1919 Military Cross; 1914/1915 Star; British War Medal; 1919 Victory medal.

Henry Spencer HADLAND (18 Feb 1889 - 28 Jul 1958), described as 6' tall, dark complexion with hazel eyes and brown hair, Church of England (*QPF Recruit Register*). Born to Charles and Blanche in New Plymouth, New Zealand. Sworn into the QPF on 2 Jul 1912, 23yrs 4mths, Reg no 1611, Roma Street station, Brisbane (QSA AF4431). Enlisted with the AIF SERN 1363 on 18 Dec 1914. Embarked with the 9th Australian Infantry Battalion aboard HMAT *Seang Bee A48* on 13 Feb 1915. Returned to Australia on 23 Sept 1918. Re-appointed to the QPF on 1 Oct 1919, 29yrs 9mths, Petrie Terrace Police Depot, Brisbane. Married Elizabeth Lizze Urmson on 7 Feb 1920 in Brisbane. Retired on 29 Jan 1939 (QSA AF4431). Died 28 Jul 1958 and buried in the Mount Thompson Memorial Gardens, Brisbane. Honours: 1914/1915 Star; British War Medal; 1919 Victory medal. Photographs: *The Queenslander Pictorial,* supplement to *The Queenslander,* 23 Jan 1915, p. 26 (SLQ Image No 702692-19150123-s0024).

James HANNIGAN (Oct 1886 – 17 Dec 1926), described as 5' 10 ½" tall, fresh complexion with brown eyes and brown hair, Roman Catholic (*QPF Recruit Register*). Born in Ireland. Served in Malay Police 30 May 1913 to 28 Feb 1914. Sworn into the QPF on 2 May 1914, 27yrs 8mths, Reg no 1860, Petrie Terrace Police Depot, Brisbane (QSA AF3258). He also served with the Irish Guards. As an Army Reservist he was called to Fort Lytton on 13 Aug 1914. He embarked on HMAT *A28 Miltiades*. Discharged on 09 Oct 1917 due to wounds caused by a burst shell injuring head and ears, which resulted in partial deafness. Returned to Australia and resumed duty with the QPF on 13 Dec 1917, Maryborough Police Station, Queensland. Resigned from the QPF on 4 Nov 1919 (QSA AF3258). Hannigan died by suicide on 17 Dec 1926, having wounded two General Post Office colleagues in Adelaide, South Australia, before shooting himself (*News*, 'Post Office Shooting', 29 Dec 1926, p. 6). Honours: 1914/1915 Star; British War Medal; 1919 Victory medal.

Michael Emmett HARTE (Oct 1885 - 1 Apr 1958), described as 5' 10" tall, dark complexion with blue eyes and brown hair, Roman Catholic (*QPF Recruit Register*). Born to John and Annie, Longford, Ireland. Served with City of Glasgow Police. Sworn into the QPF on 19 Dec 1911, 26yrs 2mths, Reg no 1531, Roma Street Station, Brisbane (QSA AF3859). Enlisted with the AIF SERN 6513 on 14 Dec 1914. Embarked with the 5th Australian Trench Mortar Battalion aboard HMAT *Minneapolis* on 20 Oct 1915. Returned to Australia on 12 Mar 1918. Resumed duty with the QPF on 12 Jul 1918, 32yrs 9mths, Sandgate Station, Brisbane. Retired 8 Oct 1927 (QSA AF3859). Died 1 Apr 1958. Honours: 1918 Military Medal (London Gazette p1403, position 56); 1914/1915 Star; British War Medal; 1919 Victory medal.

Harry Clifford HARTILL (24 May 1887 - Dec 1957), described as 5' 10" tall, fresh complexion with blue eyes and light brown hair, Church of England (*QPF Recruit Register*). Born to John and Florence in Loudon, Middlesex, England. Served with the South African Constabulary. Sworn into the QPF on 30 Apr 1909, 22yrs, Reg no 1233, Roma Street Station, Brisbane. Granted indefinite leave of absence by the Police Commissioner from 19 Apr 1914 to proceed on active service overseas with the AIF (QSA AF3218). Enlisted with the AIF SERN 506 on 24 Aug 1914. Embarked with the 11th Australian Infantry Battalion aboard HMAT *Omrah* on 3 Oct 1914. Returned to Australia on 21 Mar 1919. Resumed duty with the QPF after proving himself medically fit on 16 May 1919, Petrie Terrace Police Depot, Brisbane. Resigned 12 June 1919 to travel back to England to attend to family matters (QSA AF3218). Died Dec 1957 and buried in a Birmingham cemetery, Warwickshire, England. Honours: 1914/1915 Star; British War Medal; 1919 Victory medal.

Denis Alfred Callinan KEANE (05 June 1887 - 15 Jun 1955), described as 5' 8", fresh complexion with hazel eyes brown hair, Roman Catholic (*QPF Recruit Register*). Born to Denis and Maude in Ipswich, Queensland. Sworn into the QPF on 01 Jul 1910, 22yrs, Reg No 1348, Woolloongabba Station, Brisbane. Resigned 18 Mar 1914. Married Agnes Ellen Irwin in 1914 (QSA AF4189). Enlisted with the AIF SERN on 21 Sep 1914. Embarked with the 2nd Australian Light Horse Regiment aboard HMAT *Boorara A42* on 20 Dec 1914. Returned to Australia in 1919 (NAA Series B2455, Item 7365957). Re-appointed to the QPF on 16 Jan 1920, 31yrs, Reg no 2431, Roma Street Station, Brisbane. Retired 18 Nov 1934 (QSA AF4189). Honours: 1914/1915 Start; 1918 Military Cross (Imperial Camel Corps) on 1 Jan 1918 (*London Gazette* 11 Apr 1918, p. 4412, position 8); British War Medal. Photograph: *The Queenslander*

Pictorial, supplement to *The Queenslander*, 31 Oct 1914, p. 26 (SLQ Image No 702692-19141031-s0026-0047).

William Harold KENNY (20 Aug 1887 - 15 May 1949) - William (Bill) Harold Kenny was born on 20 August 1887, in Guyra, New South Wales to Mary Kenny (neé Moore from Wollombi) and Michael Kenny, a farmer from Kilkenny, Ireland. Bill had two sisters, Rachel and Elizabeth, as well as an older brother Henry Butler, who also served with the Queensland Police Force. In November 1917, while Bill Kenny was posted in Europe, Henry Butler Kenny (dob 27 Jan 1875) was in charge of the Warwick police during the infamous political rally. On 29 November 1917, Prime Minister Hughes was struck with an egg thrown at him from the crowd by Patrick 'Paddy' and Bart Brosnan, the Australian-born sons of Bart Brosnan from Co. Kerry. In the fallout, Prime Minister Hughes accused the local premier, and the police, of anti-conscription sentiment and disloyalty. Following an investigation by Chief Inspector Short, Senior Sergeant Kenny was exonerated of all charges. Bill's sister, Elizabeth Kenny, was a member of the Australian Army Nursing Service (AANS) and later became famous for her methods for treating the victims of poliomyelitis. Her contributions were memorialised in a biographical film eponymously titled *Sister Kenny* (1946).

Prior to joining the Queensland Police Force (QPF), Bill Kenny served with the Citizen Forces. On 28 April 1914, supernumerary Bill Kenny was sworn in with the QPF (Reg No 1852, QSA 4720), aged 26 years and 8 months. Constable Kenny was just over 6 feet tall, with brown eyes and hair, and of dark complexion. His religion is listed as 'Roman Catholic' and previous calling as a 'Farmer' (*Register of Members of the Queensland Police, 1895-1917 and 1879-1924*). Before volunteering in the Australian Imperial Force, Constable WH Kenny received only one transfer, which was Roma Street Police Station. On 21 August 1914, the day after his 27th birthday, Private Kenny was appointed to 'A' Squadron at Enoggera, Regimental Number 171 (NAA AIF B2455, Item No 11563912). On 24 September 1914, he boarded the HMAT *Star of England* from Brisbane with the 2nd Light Horse Regiment.

Pte Kenny landed in Gallipoli with the 1st Division's Mounted Military Police, 'many of whom had been recruited from men who were civil policemen and good horsemen' (*Police Bulletin*, May 2016, p. 15). According to the Royal Australian Corps of Military Police (RACMP) centenary publication, the Military Police was raised from the corps alone with a formal approval for creation of the ANZAC Provost Corps granted by General Birdwood on 9 March 1916. The order was promulgated a month later, on 3 April. In March 1915, Kenny arrived in Heliopolis and soon after was transferred to the Army Police Headquarters, where he was assigned to General Birdwood as a bodyguard.

Kenny's military record shows he was court-martialled in February 1916. The RACMP historian Geoff Barr recounts the circumstances that led to the trial:

> Early 1916, back in Egypt, Kenny was still only holding the rank of lance corporal. Towards the end of January, Lance Corporal Kenny and Trooper Patrick Delaney were involved in an incident with a group of drunken soldiers from the 14th Battalion, one of the group, a Private Thomas, swore at Kenny. Kenny dismounted and struck the soldier, who hit his head hard he fell to the ground. Kenny and Delaney then rode off, the 14th Battalion soldiers took Thomas to hospital,

where he died shortly afterwards...Court-martialled on the charge of Manslaughter, Kenny must surely have been lucky to have remained a MMP [Mounted Military Police] and to avoid being punished as a result of Thomas' death. Kenny's commendations for bravery must have assisted in his case.

Lance Corporal William Kenny, *Military discipline: policing the 1st Australian Imperial Force 1914-1920*.

On 18 May 1916, Pte Kenny was awarded "*Medaille Militaire*" by the President of the 3rd French Republic, Raymond Poincaré, in recognition for his distinguished service during the campaign. (*Com of Aus Gazette*, No 60, 18 May 1916). In June of the same year, Pte Kenny of 2nd ANZAC HQ, was awarded the Distinguished Conduct Medal 'for conspicuous good work throughout this campaign frequently under shell fire.' Mid-June, Kenny was taken ill and admitted to 24th Stationary Hospital 'suffering from mild sickness' (NAA B2455, p. 24). In July 1916, he embarked overseas with the 2nd ANZAC Police Force from Alexandria. Kenny continued to serve as a military policeman, RACMP, on the Western Front until the end of the war. His record shows he spend the rest of his service in France with three-weeks' leave in 1917. Having gradually risen through the ranks, Kenny was awarded the rank of Senior Sergeant in January 1918. In March, he had another fortnight's leave to the United Kingdom. Sr Sgt Kenny was discharged on 4 March 1919. In October 1919, Kenny married Christina Agnes McClellan. Their son William Harold was born two years later, in 1921.

Kenny resumed his police service on 8 March 1919, where he continued performing his duties for another 24 years. Constable Kenny spent 12 years in Gilbert River (1920-1932), and two years each in Tewantin, where he was in charge of the station (1932-34), Cloncurry (1934-36) and seven years in Toowoomba (1936-43). On 18 November 1927, Constable Kenny was granted a favourable record for good work in connection with the alleged stealing of calves from Oakland Park Station, near Croydon (Staff File, 843 CS). Kenny received his only promotion to Sergeant 2/c in September 1834. In November 1942, he was assaulted by Percy Richards 'whilst affecting his arrest' and sustained a fractured ankle, 'an injury that deemed him medically unfit' for police duty (10 Mar 1943, AF 4720). He retired on 5 April 1943, at the rank of Sergeant 2/c, aged 55, and continued to reside in Toowoomba at 99 MacKenzie Street. He continued working as a market gardener (NAA: B884, Q226415 p. 6). In 1937, Kenny wrote a series of articles for the *Queensland Digger*.

In 1943, Kenny re-joined the Australian Army as a Sergeant and finished a course with Australian Infantry Leaders Section qualifying as a Section Leader (NAA/ B884, Q226415 p. 5). He received one promotion in 1944, to the rank of Warrant Officer Class 1 and placed on reserve. Kenny was discharged on 21 October 1945. Bill Kenny died on 15 May 1949 of a malignant tumour of the abdomen aged 62 and is buried at Toowoomba Cemetery. The Repatriation Board accepted Kenny's cause of death as 'being due to his war service'. He was survived by his wife, Christina Agnes, and son, William Harold Kenny, an air-pilot instructor. Christina died on 13 June 1980, in Sunnybank, Brisbane. The lines at Lavarack Barracks, Townsville, are named after William Harold Kenny. Photographs: *The Queenslander Pictorial*, supplement to *The Queenslander*, 17 Oct 1914, p. 24 (SLQ Image No 702692-19141017-s0024-0049).

Thomas Henry KEMBREY (Apr 1884 - 21 Jun 1960), described as 5' 8 ¼" tall, fresh complexion with hazel eyes and brown hair, Church of England (*QPF Recruit Register*). Born to George and Helen in Gorse Hill,

Swindon, Wiltshire, England (*1891 England Census*). Sworn into the QPF on 30 Sep 1913, 28yrs 7mths, Reg no 1777, Petrie Terrace Police Depot, Brisbane (QSA AF3300). As an Imperial Reservist he reported for duty SERN 15775 on 14 Aug 1914. Embarked from Sydney with the Royal Engineers aboard HMAT *Miltiades A28* on 17 Oct 1914. Returned to Australia on 17 Sep 1919 but returned to England almost immediately to resume residence. In Dec 1919, Thomas married Eva Elizabeth Few at Swindon. Officially resigned from the QPF on 26 May 1920 (QSA AF3300). Died 21 Jun 1960 and buried in a Wiltshire Cemetery, United Kingdom. Honours: 1914/1915 Star; British War Medal; 1919 Victory medal.

William Samuel KIDDELL (28 Dec 1881 - 26 Aug 1970), described as 5' 9 ½" tall, pale complexion with grey eyes and brown hair, Church of England (*QPF Recruit Register*). Born to John and Amy in Plumstead, Kent, England. Sworn into the QPF on 24 Oct 1911, 29yrs 10mths, Reg no 1506, Petrie Terrace Police Depot, Brisbane (QSA AF4642). Enlisted with the AIF SERN on 5 Sep 1914. Embarked with the 2nd Australian Light Horse Regiment aboard HMAT *Star of England A15* on 24 Sep 1914. Returned to Australia on 11 March 1916. Discharged from AIF on 17 May 1916, after being badly wounded at Gallipoli. Married Mary McPhee at All Saints Church, Brisbane on 14 Sep 1916. Resumed QPF duty on 2 Jun 1916, 34yrs, Petrie Terrace Police Depot, Brisbane. Retired on 7 Nov 1942 (QSA AF4642). Died 26 Aug 1970 and buried in Albany Creek Memorial Park Cemetery & Crematorium, Brisbane. Honours: 1914/1915 Star. Photographs: PM0082.

George KING (5 Mar 1890 - 26 May 1935), described as 5' 8" tall, dark complexion with hazel eyes and brown hair, Church of England (*QPF Recruit Register*). Born to George and Eliza in Yandilla, Pittsworth, Queensland. Sworn into the QPF on 26 Apr 1912, 22yrs, Reg no 1585, Petrie Terrace Police Depot, Brisbane (QSA AF3094). Enlisted with the AIF SERN 414 on 4 Sep 1914. Embarked with the 2nd Australian Light Horse Regiment aboard HMAT *Star of England A15* on 24 Sep 1914. Returned to Australia on 31 Oct 1917. Re-appointed to the QPF on 18 Mar 1918, 28yrs, Petrie Terrace Police Depot, Brisbane. Resigned 30 Jun 1918 (QSA AF3094). Died 26 May 1935 in a boiler explosion, while working at a timber mill in South Brisbane (*The Courier-Mail*, 27 May 1935, p. 13). Buried in the Balmoral Cemetery, Brisbane. Honours: 16 Oct 1912 - QPF Medal for Merit; 1914/1915 Star; British War Medal; 1919 Victory medal.

Alexander Richard LANG (12 Apr 1889 - 1957), described as 5' 9" tall, fresh complexion with brown eyes and brown hair, Church of England (*QPF Recruit Register*). Born to David and Mary in Bathurst, New South Wales. Sworn into the QPF on 1 Nov 1910, 21yrs 7mths, Reg no 1375, Petrie Terrace Police Depot, Brisbane. Resigned (QSA AF3256). Enlisted with the AIF SERN 2303 on 31 Aug 1914. Embarked with the 3rd Australian Field Artillery aboard HMAT *Rangatira A22* on 25 Sep 1914. Wounded action four times and returned to Australia on 9 Feb 1919. Resigned from the QPF on 31 Oct 1919 (QSA AF3256). Died and buried in New South Wales. Honours: 1914/1915 Star; British War Medal; 1919 Victory medal.

Alfred John LOGAN (18 Jan 1886 - 03 May 1964), described as 5' 8 ¾" tall, sallow complexion with blue eyes and light brown hair, Church of England (*QPF Recruit Register*). Born to Whitmore and Harriett in Brookfield, Brisbane. Enlisted in No. 4 Squadron of the 13th Australian Light Horse on 9 Dec 1903. Sworn into the QPF on 7 Nov 1907, 21yrs, Reg no 1060, Petrie Terrace Police Depot, Brisbane. Resigned 3 Feb 1910. Re-sworn into the QPF 28 Apr 1911, 25yrs, Petrie Terrace Police Depot, Brisbane. Resigned 16 Sep 1914 (QSA AF2659). Enlisted with the AIF SERN 606 on 14 Oct 1914. Embarked with the 2nd Australian Light Horse Regiment aboard HMAT *Boorara A42* on 20 Dec 1914. Wounded at Gallipoli in the battle at Quinn's Post, Turkey in which his eldest brother, Major Thomas Logan, was killed on 7 Aug 1915. Returned to Australia on 8 Oct 1918. Re-appointed to the QPF on 1 Feb 1919, 33yrs, Reg no 1421, Petrie Terrace Police Depot, Brisbane. Married Elizabeth Martha Burnham at Forest Hill, Queensland on 19 Feb 1919. Retired 18 Jan 1946 (QSA AF2659). Died 3 May 1964 and buried in Forest Hill Cemetery, Brisbane. Honours: 1914/1915 Star; British War Medal; 1919 Victory medal. Photographs: *The Queenslander Pictorial*, supplement to *The Queenslander*, 31 Oct 1914, p. 23 (SLQ Image No 702692-19141031-s0023-0053).

Archie LUCAS (Jan 1892 - unknown), described as 5' 10 ½" tall, sallow complexion with blue eyes and fair hair, Church of England (*QPF Recruit Register*). Born to ? and Laura in East Marden, Chichester, England. Served with the 12th Middlesex Regiment for 3 years. Sworn into the QPF on 26 Apr 1912, 20yrs 4mths, Reg no 1586, Petrie Terrace Police Depot, Brisbane. Resigned 26 Sep 1914 (QSA AF2671). Enlisted with the AIF SERN 618 on 1 Oct 1914. Embarked with the 15th Australian Infantry Battalion aboard HMAT *Ceramic A40* on 22 Dec 1914. 19 May 1915 suffered fractured skull from a gunshot wound at Gallipoli, returned to Australia on 8 Oct 1915, discharged medically unfit, suffering from headaches and depression, on 2 Feb 1916 (NAA 8206834). Honours: 1914/1915 Star; British War Medal; 1919 Victory medal.

William Albert McKAY (25 Feb 1891 - 4 Aug 1955), described as 5' 10" tall, dark complexion with brown eyes and black hair, Church of England (*QPF Recruit Register*). Born to William and Margaret in May, Armagh,

Northern Ireland. Served with the Royal Garrison Artillery 03 Jun 1905 to 10 Feb 1909; the Royal Irish Constabulary 18 Jul 1910 to 11 Oct 1912; and the Durban Borough Police 15 Nov 1912 to 22 May 1913. Sworn into the QPF on 11 Dec 1913, 22yrs 9mths, Reg no 1798, Petrie Terrace Police Depot, Brisbane (QSA AF3292). Enlisted with the AIF SERN 1304 on 12 Nov 1914. Embarked with the 3rd Australian Infantry Battalion aboard HMAT *Seang Bee A48* on 11 Feb 1915. Shot in the left thigh at Gallipoli in Aug 1915 and after lengthy hospital stay, returned to Australia to convalesce on 17 Mar 1916. Returned to duty as 2nd Lieutenant on 28 Jun 1916 at the Liverpool Camp, Melbourne. Embarked with the 45th Australian Battalion aboard HMAS Marathon on 9 May 1917. Returned to Australia on 1 Nov 1919. William's AIF appointment was terminated on 15 Feb 1920 and his resignation from the QPF was dated the same day. Died 4 Aug 1955 in Omagh, Tyrone, Northern Ireland. Honours: 1914/1915 Star; British War Medal; 1919 Victory medal.

Charles Ian McLEAN (15 Sep 1891 - 22 Jan 1967), described as 5' 9½" tall, fresh complexion with brown eyes and black hair, Presbyterian (*QPF Recruit Register*). Born to Charles and Margaret in County Galway, Ireland. Arrived in Australia on 19 May 1911 on SS *Pakeha*. Sworn into the QPF on 6 Oct 1911, 20yrs 1mth, Reg no 1499, Petrie Terrace Police Depot, Brisbane. Resigned 7 Oct 1914 (QSA AF3742). Enlisted with the AIF SERN 958 on 27 Dec 1914. Embarked with the 2nd Australian Light Horse Regiment aboard HMAT *Malakuta A57* on 22 May 1915. Returned to Australia on 9 Jul 1919 (NAA Feb3004604). Resumed duty with the QPF on 9 Oct 1919, Petrie Terrace Police Depot, Brisbane. Resigned 31 Aug 1925 (QSA AF3742). Appointed European Constable, Port Moresby 26 May 1927, and an officer of the Armed Constabulary 4 Aug 1927. His contract was terminated 25 Feb 1929. Died 22 Jan 1967.

Honours: 1914/1915 Star; British War Medal; 1919 Victory medal; 1925 Kings Police Medal.

Henry Michael McLEAN (02 Jun 1886 - 10 Sep 1917 KIA), described as 5' 10" tall, fresh complexion with blue eyes and brown hair, Church of England (*QPF Recruit Register*). Born to ? and Ellen in Dublin, Ireland. Served with the Irish Guards before emigrating. Sworn into the QPF on 2 Sep 1913, 27yrs 3mths, Reg no 1764, Roma Street Station, Brisbane (QS AF3100). He reported for duty on 9 Aug 1914, as an Imperial Reservist, SERN 2396. Embarked with the 1st Battalion Irish Guards aboard HMAT *Militades A28* on 17 Oct 1914. Killed by shellfire on the afternoon of 10 Sep 1917, in the vicinity of Langemark, Belgium during the Battle of Passchendaele. Henry's body was never recovered (NAA Series MT1487/1 Item 6044352). Memorialised on the Tyne Cot Memorial Wall, Ypres, Belgium. Honours: British War Medal; 1919 Victory medal. Killed in action.

Alexander McLEOD (5 Jul 1890 - unknown), described as 5' 11 ¾" tall, fair complexion with blue eyes and fair hair, Presbyterian (*QPF Recruit Register*). Born to Murdoch Roderick and Margaret in Duirinish, Inverness, Scotland. Sworn into the QPF on 8 Aug 1911, 21yrs, Reg no 1480, Roma Street Station, Brisbane. Resigned on 6 Oct 1914 (QSA AF3441). Enlisted with the AIF SERN 285 on 9 Sep 1914. Embarked with the 9th Australian Infantry Battalion aboard HMAT *Omrah A5* on 24 Sep 1914. Returned to Australia on 15 Aug 1915. Discharged from the AIF as medically unfit suffering from rheumatism sciatica on 25 Nov 1915. Re-sworn into the QPF on 18 Dec 1916, Reg No 2226, Cunnamulla Station, Queensland. Resigned 31 Dec 1921. Honours: 1914/1915 Star; British War Medal; 1919 Victory medal.

Thomas MORRIS (3 Jan 1892 - 22 Aug 1941), described as 5' 11 ½" tall, sallow complexion with brown eyes and fair hair, Roman Catholic (*QPF Recruit Register*). Born in Brisbane Queensland. Sworn into the QPF on 6 Oct 1911, 19yrs, Reg no 1498, Petrie Terrace Police Depot, Brisbane. Resigned 9 Jul 1914 (QSA AF3737). Enlisted with the AIF SERN 508 on 21 Aug 1914. Embarked with the 9th Australian Battalion aboard HMAT *Omrah A5* on 24 Sep 1914. Repatriated to Australia suffering from a hernia on 29 Jul 1915. Discharged from the AIF on 8 Oct 1915 (NAA: Series B2455, Item 7988535). Attempted to re-join the QPF but was found unfit for duty. After a hernia operation he re-enlisted with the AIF SERN 3046 on 17 Jul 1916. Embarked with the 47th Australian Battalion aboard *Marathon A74* on 27 Oct 1916. On 18 Jan 1918 near Bellenglise, France, he received gunshot wound to right foot and was repatriated to Australia on 15 Jan 1919 and discharged from the AIF on 16 Apr 1919. Re-appointed to the QPF on 16 Jun 1919, Reg no 2407, Petrie Terrace Police Depot, Brisbane. Dismissed on 5 Aug 1925, for being on licensed premises in the Crown Hotel, Cairns without lawful cause (QSA AF3737). Married Alice Lucy McMullen (nee' O'SHEA) on 20 Oct 1928. Died 22 Aug 1941 at the Dunwich Benevolent Asylum and buried in plot in the Toowong Cemetery, Brisbane. Honours: 1914/1915 Star; British War Medal; 1919 Victory medal.

Patrick James MOYNIHAN (19 Aug 1888 - 25 Apr 1915 KIA), was born in Allora, Queensland to Patrick and Kate, neé Carolan (also Catherine Carolin) (Reg 1888/C/2655). Patrick James had 10 siblings, 8 girls and 4 boys; two of the children died in infancy.

Before joining the Queensland Police Force on 20 February 1913, Moynihan worked on the railways at Wallangarra for two and a half years. In April, Supernumerary Moynihan had to be hospitalised with typhoid fever, which extended his training period by over a month. He was sworn in on 4 July 1913 (Reg no 1749). He is listed as 5 feet 9 ¾ inches tall, measuring 40 inches across the chest, of ruddy complexion with fair hair and blue eyes, Roman Catholic (*QPF Recruit Register*). He was single upon entry. His policing career was brief with only one transfer, and he was stationed at Fortitude Valley, Brisbane (AF2967; AF1161).

Constable Moynihan enlisted in the AIF (SERN 1130) on 17 October 1914, and assigned to 9th infantry Battalion, 1st Reinforcement. The 9th Battalion was among the first infantry units to be raised for the AIF during the First World War. It was also the first battalion recruited in Queensland, and along with the 10th, 11th and 12th Battalions it formed the 3rd Brigade. The battalion was raised within weeks of the declaration of the war in August 1914, and just two months later embarked in stages. Private Moynihan boarded His Majesty's Australian Transport (HMAT) *A32 Themistocles* on the 22 December 1914 in Melbourne bound for Egypt (NAA 7985473, p. 21).

On 9 February 1915, Private Moynihan arrived at Mena Camp, joining the 9th Battalion for training. The British Expeditionary Forces (BEF) were then assembled at Lemnos. On 25 April 1915, as the covering force for the ANZAC landing, the 3rd Brigade was the first ashore at around 4:30 in the morning. The battalion was heavily involved in establishing and defending the front line of the ANZAC beachhead (*The Fighting Ninth: Official Journal of the 9th Battalion*, 1947, SLQ S 355 009).

MOYNIHAN's 14th platoon was taken as close to shore as possible on the Destroyer HMS 'Colne' before it manned the boats to row the remaining distance to shore. MOYNI-

HAN's Company had landed on the right flank as intended but the rest of the 3rd Brigade landed hopelessly intermingled. To add to the confusion, they were all landed a mile further north than had been planned. Undeterred by the setback, they followed their orders and headed inland, with MOYNIHAN's company climbing McKays Hill to the 400 Plateau. Gaba Tepe was now too far away but they could see the third ridge. Small groups fought their way across the scrubby plateau underneath a hail of Turkish shrapnel and Moynihan is believed to have been one of the 9th Battalion men, who advanced to the Third Ridge with Lt LOUTIT of the 11th Battalion. This group was forced into a desperate fighting withdrawal back to 400 Plateau, due to the Turkish counterattack around 10:00 on the day of the landing.

Paul Ruge, *Their Glory Shall Not be Blotted Out*, 2006.

According to Joseph Moynihan's statement, his brother Patrick James 'was among the first to make the landing at Anzac Cove on the morning of 25/4/15 and with a great many others advanced overfar towards the Narrows. It was then found necessary to retreat and in the retreat he was supposed to have been shot in the head but his mates had not had time to obtain his identification disc' (NAA 7985473). He was initially listed as 'Missing in Action' as he sustained a gunshot to the head on the Turkish side of the frontline and his body was never recovered.

Following the inquiry and official confirmation of Patrick's death, Joseph Moynihan lodged a request to receive the military honours on behalf of his brother. However, he was informed that as the closest living relative, Patrick's daughter was to receive the medals. Mary Malcolm Cameron was born on 12 June 1915. This came as a surprise to the family. It is likely Patrick himself did not know his intended, Ruby Cameron, was pregnant when he left Australia in December 1914. Mary lived with her mother in Greenslopes, a Brisbane's inner-city suburb. Patrick's AIF records show Ruby was awarded Pte Moynihan's military pension. Mary had type 1 diabetes and died on 30 December 1928, aged only 13 years (NAA 7985473, p. 27). Ruby lived to 89 years and died in 1980 (11 Apr 1891 – 18 Nov 1980).

On 6 November 1995, the Queensland Police vessel was commissioned and officially named *P. J. MOYNIHAN* by Police Minister Paul Braddy. Constable Moynihan's closest living relative, his nephew's widow Catherine Moynihan of Kallangur (north of Brisbane) attended the ceremony. The vessel is a Haines Hunter 680 SF (Hull Number 337), 6.8 metre glass reinforced fibre speed boat, powered by a single 250 HP Johnson Outboard Motor. It is attached to the Wynnum District Water Police (http://www.qldwaterpolice.com/Bio/P_J_Moynihan.html). Moynihan is memorialised at Lone Pine Memorial, Panel 31, Gallipoli Peninsula, Canakkale Province, Turkey. Honours: British War Medal, Victory Medal, Memorial Plaque, Memorial Scroll. Photographs: PM0111, PM2227. Killed in action.

Phillip O'BRIEN (20 Jul 1892 - 7 May 1915), described as 5' 10 ½" tall, dark complexion with brown eyes and black hair, Roman Catholic (*QPF Recruit Register*). Born to James and Dora in Beaudesert, Queensland. Sworn into the QPF on 1 Oct 1910, 18yrs 2mths, Reg no 1369, Petrie Terrace Police Depot, Brisbane. Resigned 30 Sep 1912 (QSA AF2414). Enlisted with the AIF SERN 183 on 22 Aug 1914. Embarked with the 9th Australian Infantry Battalion aboard HMT *Omrah A5* on 24 Sep 1914. Sustained a shrapnel wound to the right knee at Gallipoli and died of this wound on 7 May 1915, aboard HMAT *Lutzow* and was buried at sea. Remembered at Lone Pine Memorial, Gallipoli Peninsula, Canakkale Province, Turkey. Honours: 1914/1915 Star; British War Medal; 1919 Victory medal.

Thomas Charles O'LOUGHLIN (Jan 1893 - 15 Oct 1932), described as 5' 8" tall, fresh complexion with blue eyes and fair hair, Roman Catholic (*QPF Recruit Register*). Born to Patrick and Mary in Ballarat, Victoria. Sworn into the QPF on 6 Nov 1912, 19yrs 10mths, Reg no 1676, South Brisbane Station, Brisbane (QSA AF3096). Enlisted with the AIF SERN 786 on 26 Dec 1914. Embarked with the 5th Australian Light Horse Regiment aboard HMAT *Itria A53* on 9 Feb 1915. Invalided back to Australia on 3 Jan 1916, for three months to recover from recurrent gonorrhoea and typhoid fever. Re-joined the AIF SERN 1204 on 26 May 1916 and proceeded with the 67th Australian Battalion to France on 16 Nov 1916. Wounded in action 31 Jan 1917 and sent back to France on 25 Aug 1917, having been reassigned to the 39th Battalion as a reinforcement. He suffered a severe gunshot wound to the head and a fractured skull on 4 Oct 1917, invalided to Australia on 15 Feb 1918, discharged from the AIF medically unfit on 20 Jun 1918. Died 15 Oct 1932 and buried in the Victoria Garden of Remembrance, Springvale, Greater Dandenong City, Victoria. Honours: 1914/1915 Star; British War Medal; 1919 Victory medal.

Ernest Richard PASTORELLI (31 Dec 1884 - 12 Oct 1918 KIA), described as 5' 8 ¼" tall, dark complexion with blue eyes and brown hair, Church of England (*QPF Recruit Register*). Born in Brixton, Middlesex, England (QSA AF3212). Sworn into the QPF on 23 May 1911, 26yrs 5mths, Reg no 1436, Roma Street Station (QSA AF3212). As a British Military Reservist, he was recalled to active army duty on 20 Aug 1914 as part of "A" Battery, 156th Brigade, Royal Field Artillery SERN 39702. Captured and died as prisoner of war at Lagensala War Hospital Camp (German Prisoner of War Camp) from dropsy caused by exhaustion on 12 Oct 1918. Buried in Niederzwehren Cemetery, Germany. Honours: 1914/1915 Star; British War Medal; 1919 Victory medal. Killed in action.

William Joseph POWER (9 Dec 1889 - 6 May 1956), described as 5' 8 ½" tall, fresh complexion with hazel eyes and brown hair, Roman Catholic (*QPF Recruit Register*). Born to William and Mary in Stanthorpe, Queensland. Sworn into the QPF 1 Mar 1909, 19yrs 2mths, Reg no 1216, Sandgate Station, Brisbane. Resigned 16 Jul 1914 (QSA AF2640). Enlisted with the AIF SERN 488 on 6 Oct 1914. Promoted to Corporal and embarked with the 2nd Australian Light Horse Field Ambulance. Returned to Australian 23 Dec 1918. Died 6 May 1956 at Gumdale, Queensland and buried in plot 8-15-11 in the Anzac section of the Lutwyche Cemetery.

James RAFTER (22 Jun 1885 - 13 Sep 1954), described as 5' 9" tall, fair complexion with blue eyes and brown hair, Roman Catholic (*QPF Recruit Register*). Born to John and Carolyn in Morven, Queensland. Sworn into the QPF on 16 May 1907, 21yrs, Reg no 1006, Petrie Terrace Police Depot, Brisbane. Resigned 18 Mar 1914 (QSA AF2588). Enlisted with the AIF SERN 9 on 21 Aug 1914. Embarked with the 2nd Australian Light Horse Regiment aboard HMAT *Star of England A15* on 24 Sep 1914. Returned to Australia on 7 Jan 1919. Re-appointed to the QPF on 9 Feb 1920, 35yrs, Reg no 2442, Rewan Police Horse Stud, Brisbane. Retired on 22 Jun 1945 (QSA AF2588). Died 13 Sep 1954 and buried in plot 7A-176-2 at Toowong Cemetery, Brisbane. Honours: 1914/1915 Star; British War Medal; 1919 Victory medal.

Greville James SMITH (29 May 1891 - 7 Oct 1972), described as 6' tall, ruddy complexion with blue eyes and fair hair, Presbyterian (*QPF Recruit Register*). Born to William and Harriet in Esk, Queensland. Sworn into the QPF on 1 Oct 1914, 23yrs 4mths, Reg no 1927, Petrie Terrace Police Depot, Brisbane (QSA AF5628). Enlisted with the AIF SERN 482 on 5 Nov 1914. Embarked with the 5th Australian Light Horse Regiment aboard HMAT *Persic A34* on 21 Dec 1914. Severely wounded on 17 Jul 1917, left leg amputated 23 Oct 1917. Returned to Australia on 30 Jun 1918. Resumed QPF duty on 14 Jan 1919, Reg no 1927, Roma Street Station (Telephone Attendant), Brisbane. Retired on 29 May 1951 (QSA AF5628). Died 7 Oct 1972. Honours: 1914/1915 Star; British War Medal; 1918 Military Medal for gallantry in action and devotion to duty; 1919 Victory medal. Photographs: PM4557.

Benjamin William SUTHERLAND (4 Jul 1888 - unknown), described as 5' 9" tall, fair complexion with brown eyes and fair hair, Presbyterian (*QPF Recruit Register*). Born in Wick, Caithness, Scotland. Served in the Liverpool City Police between 12 Oct 1908 and 5 Jan 1912. Served 12 months with the Seaforth Highlanders Volunteers and was also attached to the Territorial Force of Scotland for 12 months. Sworn into the QPF on 8 Jul 1914, 26yrs, Reg no 1878, Roma Street Station, Brisbane (QSA AF3195). Enlisted with the AIF SERN 73 on 8 Sep 1914. Embarked with the 3rd Field Ambulance aboard HMAT *Rangatira A22* on 25 Sep 1914. Returned to Australia on 23 October 1918. Resigned from the QPF on 19 Mar 1919 to take up a selection at Cecil Plains (QSA AF3195). Honours: 1914/1915 Star; British War Medal; 1919 Victory medal.

Ernest Leslie THOMSON (6 Jun 1882 - 5 Jun 1947), described as 5' 10 ¾" tall, fresh complexion with brown eyes and brown hair, Presbyterian (*QPF Recruit Register*). Born to George and Ellen in Pittsworth,

Queensland. Sworn into the QPF on 11 Feb 1914, 30yrs 8mths, Reg no 1819, Petrie Terrace Police Depot, Brisbane. Resigned 22 Aug 1914 (QSA AF2654). Enlisted with the AIF SERN 1005 on 14 Sep 1914. Embarked with the 9th Australian Infantry Battalion aboard HMAT *Omrah A5* on 24 Sep 1914. Returned to Australia on 24 Sep 1918 (NAA 1837763). Died 5 Jun 1947 and buried in plot 7-80-39, Anzac Section, Lutwyche Cemetery, Kedron, Brisbane. Honours: 1914/1915 Star; British War Medal; 1919 Victory medal.

Phillip Charles VOWLES (Aug 1887 - 02 Oct 1915 KIA), described as 5′ 8 ¾″ tall, dark complexion with brown eyes and brown hair, Church of England (*QPF Recruit Register*). Born in Bristol, England. Sworn into the QPF on 26 Apr 1912, 25yrs 9mths, Reg no 1599, Woolloongabba Station (QS AF2666). Enlisted in the AIF SERN 996 on 20 Aug 1914. Embarked with the 9th Australian Infantry Battalion aboard HMAT *Omrah A5* on 24 Sep 1914. After the first Gallipoli offensive, Lance Corporal Vowles succumbed to illness on 8 Sep, admitted to ANZAC hospital with influenza which developed into dysentery and pneumonia. Transferred first to Imbros, Turkey and then to Netley Military Hospital, England. Died from pneumonia on 2 Oct 1915. Buried in the Netley Military Cemetery, Hamble-le-Rice, England (NAA 8398575). Honours: 1914/1915 Star; British War Medal. Killed in action.

Edward WALSH (Mar 1892 - 24 Jun 1915 KIA), described as 6′ tall, dark complexion with hazel eyes and brown hair, Roman Catholic (*QPF Recruit Register*). Born to John and Honoria in Castlebar, Ireland. Sworn into the QPF on 29 Jan 1912, 19yrs 10mths, Reg no 1567, Petrie Terrace Police Depot, Brisbane. Resigned 26 Sep 1914 (QSA AF2669). Enlisted with the AIF SERN 1812 on 2 Oct 1914. Embarked with the 301 Mechanical Transport aboard HMAT *Ceramic A40* on 22 Dec 1914. Died 24

Jun 1915 aged 23 of shell wounds received to his head, neck, mouth and chest at Gallipoli. Buried in the Ari Burnu Cemetery, Gallipoli Peninsula, Canakkale Province, Turkey. Honours: 1914/1915 Star. Killed in Action.

Alex WATSON (17 Jul 1893 - 30 Jun 1916 KIA), described as 5' 8" tall, dark complexion with brown hair and brown eyes, Church of England (*QPF Recruit Register*). Born to Kirby and Mary in Maroon, Boonah, Queensland. Sworn into the QPF on 2 Jul 1912, 19yrs, Reg no 1625, Rosewood Station, Brisbane. Dismissed 13 Jan 1914 (QSA AF2548). Enlisted into AIF SERN 245 on 26 Aug 1914. Embarked in September with the 9th Australian Infantry Battalion aboard HMAT *Omrah A5* on 24 Sep 1914. Returned to Australia 4 May 1915 suffering from gonorrhoea. Re-enlisted into AIF in Victoria SERN 1593 on 22 Jun 1915. Embarked with the 24th Australian Infantry Battalion aboard HMAS Euripides on 10 Jul 1915. Alex Watson was killed in action during a trench raid around Armentieres on 30 Jun 1916, his body was brough back from the front and buried in the Ration Farm Military Cemetery, La Chapelle-D'armentieres, Lille, Nord Pas de Calais, France. Photographs: PM42124. Killed in Action.

Edward William WRIGHT (11 Jan 1883 - 19 Aug 1968), described as 5' 8" tall, dark complexion with brown eyes and dark hair, Presbyterian (*QPF Recruit Register*). Born to Emmanuel and Francis O'Connell in Oxley, Queensland. Sworn into the QPF on 23 Jan 1908, 25 years, Reg no 1095, Roma Street Station (QSA AF3483). Married Laura Johansen 11 Jun 1912, Springsure. Enlisted into the AIF SERN 475 on 16 Oct 1914, refused permission to take 'leave of absence' due to staff shortage, resigned 31 Oct 1914. Embarked with 5th Light Horse regiment from Sydney on HMAT *Vestalia A44* on 19 Dec 1914. Served in Egypt, twice invalided in England with dysentery, sent home to Australia to recover. Re-embarked as a Gunner in 49th Battery on the 4 Sep 1918 aboard HMAT *Bakara*. Returned to Brisbane 26 Mar 1919 on HMAT *Carmia* (NAA 3447432). Re-appointed to QPF on 24 Mar 1919, Reg no 2393, Mackay Station, Queensland (QSA AF3483). Resigned 14 Jun 1922. Died 19 Aug 1968, buried in plot 3-17-32 in the Mackay City Cemetery. Honours: 1914/1915 Star; British War Medal; 1919 Victory medal.

1915

Samuel Charles ADERMANN (08 Dec 1891 - 13 Aug 1986), described as 5' 9" tall, dark complexion with brown eyes and black hair, Baptist (*QPF Recruit Register*). Born to Charles and Emilee, Vernor, Queensland. Sworn into the QPF on 1 Feb 1913, 20yrs 2mths, Reg No 1697, Roma Street Station, Brisbane (QSA AF5689). Married Edith Jane Pritchard on 13 May 1915 (Australian Marriage Index Reg No B 017705). Enlisted with the AIF SERN 3678 on 30 Aug 1915. Embarked with the 9th Australian Infantry Battalion aboard HMAT *Itonus A50* on 30 Dec 1915. Returned to Australia on 1 May 1919. Reappointed to the QPF on 1 Aug 1919, 26yrs 9mths, Roma Street Station, Brisbane (*QPF Recruit Register*). Widowed 14 Dec 1933. Married Hertha Sturm on 13 Feb 1937. Retired 8 Dec 1951. Died 13 Aug 1986 and buried in plot 29-39-24 in Toowong Cemetery, Brisbane (*QPF Recruit Register*). Honours: 1914/1915 Star; 1919 British War medal; 1919 Victory Medal. Photographs: *The Queenslander Pictorial*, supplement to *The Queenslander,* 08 Apr 1916, p. 25 (SLQ Image No 702692-19160408-s0025-001).

Albert Edward BAILEY (Jul 1890 - 01 Sep 1978), described as 5' 8 ¼" tall, fresh complexion, brown eyes and brown hair, Methodist (*QPF Recruit Register*). Born to James and Caroline, Dartford, Swanscombe, England. Sworn into the QPF on 1 Feb 1913, 22yrs 6mths, Reg No 1698, Roma Street Station, Brisbane (QSA AF3229). Enlisted with the AIF

SERN 3493 on 16 January 1915. Embarked with 7th Australian Field Ambulance aboard HMAT *Ascanius A11* on 24 May 1915. Returned to Australia on 6 May 1919. Resigned from the QPF on 18 Jul 1919. Died 1 Sep 1978 and buried in plot E01353 in the Esk Cemetery, Queensland. Honours: 1914/1915 Star; 1919 British War Medal; 1919 Victory Medal.

Michael Joseph BERGIN (05 Mar 1885 - 05 Jan 1958), described as 5' 11 ¼" tall, fresh complexion with brown eyes and brown hair, Roman Catholic (*QPF Recruit Register*). Born to Michael and Mary, Castlemarket, County Kilkenny, Ireland. Sworn into the QPF on 1 Jul 1910, 25yrs 4mths, Reg no 1344, Toowoomba Station (QSA AF4015). Enlisted with the AIF SERN 10051 on 15 Sep 1915. Embarked with the 7th Australian Field Ambulance aboard the HMAT *Star of Victoria A16* on 31 Mar 1916. Returned to Australia 12 Jun 1919. Resumed duty with the QPF on 4 Sep 1919, 32yrs, South Brisbane Station, Brisbane. Retired 16 Nov 1930 (QSA AF4015). Died 5 Jan 1958, buried in plot T-32M of the South Brisbane Cemetery. Honours: Queensland 1913 Police Medal for Merit; 1914 Royal Humane Society's Certificate of Merit; 1914/1915 Star; 1919 British War Medal; 1919 Victory Medal.

Stephen Lewis BIDDINGTON (Nov 1884 - 30 May 1950), described as 5' 11 ¼" tall, dark complexion with brown eyes and brown hair, Wesleyan (*QPF Recruit Register*). Born to Stephen and Florence, Bellair, Natal, South Africa. Served 2yrs 6mths with South African colonial forces during the Boer War. Sworn into the QPF on 1 Nov 1908, 24yrs, Reg No 1172, Police Depot, Brisbane. Married Florence Emily Gardiner on 26 Apr 1911 without Commissioner's approval and subsequently discharged from the QPF on 4 May 1911 (QSA AF 3073). His son Victor Lewis was born 11 Sep 1911. Enlisted with AIF SERN 602 on 21 Oct 1915. Embarked with 4th Infantry Battalion aboard HMAT *Te Anau* on 20 Nov 1915.

Returned to Australia 26 Feb 1917 (NAA 3080616). Re-appointed to QPF on 2 Jul 1917, 33yrs, Reg No 2274, Hughenden Police Station. Dismissed on 25 Oct 1917 (*QPF Recruit Register*). Died 30 May 1950. Honours: 1914/1915 Star; British War medal; 1919 Victory Medal.

William Edwin BISHOP (Oct 1891 - 05 Nov 1916 KIA) described as 5' 10 ¾" tall, ruddy complexion with brown eyes and brown hair, Church of England (*QPF Recruit Register*). Born to James and Alice, Bristol, England. Serving for two years in Gloucester Regiment of the 6th Battalion Territorials. Sworn into the QPF on 26 Nov 1912, 21yrs 1mth, Reg no 1684, Roma Street Station (QSA AF2941). Enlisted in the AIF SERN 2118 on 5 Aug 1915. Embarked with the 25th Australian Infantry Battalion aboard HMAT Armadale A26 on 18 Sep 1915. Killed by machine gun fire on 5 Nov 1916 at the Somme, France. Memorialised in the Villers-Bretonneux Memorial, Villers-Bretonneux, Picardie, France. Honours: 1914/1915 Star; 1919 British War Medal; 1919 Victory Medal; Photographs: PM4560. Killed in action.

Arthur Albert BOCK (10 Sep 1883 - 11 May 1966) Arthur Albert Bock was born on 10 September 1883, in Bendley, South Australia to Australian-born Gottlieb Reinhold and Johanne Caroline Shilling. His mother's family, Johann Gottfried and Anna Rosina Lange, immigrated from Brandenburg, Prussia (*Genealogie Online Trees Index, 1000-2015* Netherlands). Arthur came from a large Protestant family; he had an older brother, Ernest Theodore, and 5 younger sisters (Edith Emelia, Alice Julie, Hilda Myrtle, Wilhelmina May and Susan Elizabeth) and a younger brother, Hurtle George. Susan Elizabeth, born in 1884, died only a few months old (*Australia, Birth Index*, 1788-1922, 555, p. 251).

On 3 May 1904, at 21 years old, Bock was appointed to the Queensland Police Force as a trial candidate (Reg No 467, QSA File 4759). The Register describes Arthur as 5 feet 10 inches tall, with blue eyes, fair hair, and of fresh complexion. His religion is listed as 'Church of England' and previous calling as a 'Labourer'. (*Register of Members of the Queensland Police, 1895-1917 and 1879-1924*). Bock was sworn in on 1 October. Between 1904 and 1915, Constable Bock received numerous transfers. He was stationed at Roma Street, Charters Towers, Croydon, Toowoomba, Pittsworth and Oxley stations. In 1909, five years after joining the QPF, Bock married Annie Atkinson. They resided in Hunter Street, Indooroopilly. By June 1915, Bock was an experienced and competent policeman, and a father of three young children.

On 22 June 1915, at nearly 32-years old, Bock volunteered with the AIF, the 25th Battalion. On 3 January 1916, Private Bock embarked on HMAT *Kyarra*, Brisbane for Marseilles, France (NAA B2455). In May 1916, he joined 8th Battalion. In July, he was shot in action in his right thigh and admitted to the General Hospital in Calais, France. Three days later, Bock embarked on *Newhaven* for England and was readmitted to Fifth Northern General Hospital. In November, following a four-months' recovery period, he proceeded back to France. At the end of 1916, Private Bock received his first promotion to Temporary Corporal, and in 1917, he joined No 4 Officers Cadet 9th Battalion.

Following his promotion to 2nd Lieutenant in June, he was posted to General Infantry Reinforcements. A month later, he was sent back to France and then Belgium. At Polygon Wood, Westhoe Ridge he was shot again and evacuated to War Hospital, Epsom, both his legs severely wounded. On 23 October 1917, Bock was promoted to Lieutenant. A week prior, on 14 October 1917, he was awarded the Military Cross for his actions at Westhoe Ridge, Belgium:

HIS MAJESTY THE KING has been pleased to confer the Military Cross on the undermentioned Officer for gallantry and distinguished service in the field:

Second Lieutenant ARTHUR ALBERT BOCK

For the conspicuous gallantry and devotion to duty. Whilst leading his platoon this officer encountered a series of concrete dug-outs. He rushed the entrance of one, and, single-handed, captured 17 prisoners. He continued to lead his platoon until severely wounded in both legs, setting a splendid example of coolness and daring to all ranks.

Extract from the *Commonwealth Australian Gazette, No 19, 14 Feb 1918*

On 30 January 1918, Bock embarked on A14 for Australia, as his health was deteriorating. The official reason was listed as 'GSW Both Thighs Old Thrombosis [thrombosis of femoral artery]' (NAA B2455). In May 1918, Department of Defence Melbourne, recommended that Lieutenant Bock, MC 25th Battalion, be terminated from the Australian Military Forces on medical grounds. Ernest Theodore, Arthur's older brother, also volunteered to fight in the First World War with the New Zealand Army.

He joined in June 1916 and was killed in action on 12 September 1918 in France (Field Service, NZA 29609).

Bock returned to Brisbane and in May 1918, resumed police duty. Senior Constable Bock was first stationed at Toogoolawah, then Sandgate, Barcaldine, Longreach, Fortitude Valley and Roma Street stations. In the 1920s, he organised and commanded a staff of plain clothes police at Roma St Headquarters. By the 1930s, Bock rose to the rank of inspector and was awarded numerous favourable records. In January 1927, he was awarded a favourable record for 'good work performed in conjunction with other Police in connection with the arrest and conviction of Harry Collins; William Hy Power; etc., for the theft of £145 from QN Bank, Brisbane' (*QPG* Jan 1927, QPF Service History). In 1932, Sub Inspector Bock was granted a reward of £25 by the Arson Award Agreement for good work, in conjunction with other police in connection with the conviction of Mrs Jane Campbell for arson at Bowen Hills. Inspector Bock retired from the Queensland Police on 10 September 1943 (*Brisbane Courier*, 9 Sep 1943, p. 4).

Arthur and Annie Bock went on to have five children: Ronald Atkinson Bock, Dulcie Jean Peterson (neé Bock), Olga Ruth Lang, Lillian Edith McIver, and Hurtle Arthur Bock. Dulcie Jean (dob 22 Aug 1920), joined the Queensland Police as a probationary Policewoman (19WP) in March 1946, and her appointment was confirmed a year later. The first women were employed by the Queensland Police in 1931. They were assigned heavily gendered functions, such as making general inquiries regarding women and children, escorting them to and from courts. Policewomen regularly patrolled parks and streets, theatre and hotel lounges watching for young people or children loitering or truanting from school. They advised 'delinquent' girls in connection with their conduct, mode of living, and when necessary, assisted in securing employment such as in instances of unmarried mothers. PWs did not carry weapons or have full powers of arrest and retained a probationary status for the entire duration of employment in the force (AF5496). Prior to joining the police, Dulcie served for 3 years and 10 months as a Sergeant Stenographer in the Australian Women's Army Service during the Second World War, based out of Land Headquarters in Melbourne. She married Constable Victor Henry Peterson in 1948 and resigned from the force in August 1950.

Arthur Albert Bock died on 11 May 1966 from cerebral haemorrhage at the Repatriation Hospital, Greenslopes. Photographs: PM0792, PM2031; *Brisbane Courier*, 9 Sep 1943, p. 4; PM1480 (Dulcie); *The Queenslander Pictorial* supplement to *The Queenslander*, 17 Nov 1917, p. 28 (SLQ Image No 702692-19171117-s0028-0001).

David Christopher BOURKE (31 May 1888 - 02 May 1915 KIA), described as 5' 10 ¼" tall, fresh complexion, blue eyes and brown hair, Roman Catholic (*QPF Recruit Register*). Born to Patrick and Catherine, Irvinestown, Fermanagh, Ireland (*1901 Scotland Census*). Member of the Royal Irish Constabulary between 15 Oct 1907 and 17 Oct 1912 (RIC 1310). Sworn into the QPF on 11 Feb 1914, 25yrs 8mths, Reg no 1802, South Brisbane Station (QSA AF2768). Enlisted in AIF SERN 1310 on 13 Jan 1915. Embarked with the 15th Australian Infantry Battalion aboard HMAT *Seang Bee A48* on 12 Feb 1915. Wounded in action at the Dardanelles (Gallipoli) and admitted to the Government Hospital at Alexandria, Egypt on 1 May 1915 (NAA 3100776). Succumbed to his wounds on 2 May 1915. Buried in the Chatby Military and War Memorial Cemetery, Alexandria, Egypt. Honours: 1914/1915 Star; 1919 British War Medal; 1919 Victory Medal; Photographs: *The Queenslander Pictorial* supplement to *The Queenslander,* 24 Oct 1914, p. 22 (SLQ Image No 702692-19141024-s0022). Killed in action.

Patrick Joseph BROWNE (17 Jul 1891 - 08 Jul 1925), described as 5' 8 1/4" tall, fresh complexion with blue eyes and brown hair, Roma Catholic (*QPF Recruit Register*). Born to ? and Julia, Bantry, County Cork, Ireland. Sworn into the QPF on 28 Apr 1914, 22yrs 9mths, Reg no 1845, Roma Street Station, Brisbane. Dismissed 15 Sep 1915 (QSA AF2809). Enlisted with the AIF SERN 3775 on 21 Sep 1915. Embarked with the 49th Australian Infantry Battalion aboard HMAT *Wandilla A62* on 31 Jan 1916. Returned to Australia on 10 Dec 1918 suffering from mild shell shock (NAA 3131386). Found dead on 8 Jul 1925 in Lewis and Company's Engineering Works shed, near Davies Park, West End (QSA AF2809). Honours: British War Medal; 1919 Victory medal.

Donald Alexander CAMPBELL (26 Jun 1888 – 02 Aug 1976), described as 5' 8 ½", fresh complexion with blue eyes and brown hair, Presbyterian (*QPF Recruit Register*). Born to John and Margaret (McKinnon), Glenorchy, Scotland. Sworn into the QPF on 26 Apr 1912, 23yrs 9mths, Reg no 1575, South Brisbane Station (QSA AF4851). Enlisted with the AIF SERN 594 on 13 Jan 1915. Embarked with the 25th Australian Battalion aboard HMAT *Aeneas* on 29 Jun 1915. Reported missing in action 14 Nov 1916. Officially reported as a prisoner of war, wounded in the hand and foot, captured at Serres Grebsen from Cambrai on 13 Nov 1916. Repatriated 17 Dec 1918 to London. Returned to Australia on the Port Denison on 19 May 1919 and discharged 18 Jul 1919 (Enlistment paperwork). Re-appointed with the QPF, 31yrs, North Ipswich Station (QSA AF4851). Retired 3 Oct 1945. Died on 02 1976 and buried at the Mount Thompson Memorial Gardens (QLD Death Reg No 1976/B/71074). Honours: 1916 mentioned in despatches for good services rendering Routine Orders 1st Anzac; 1914/1915 Star; 1921 British War Medal; 1919 Victory Medal. Photograph: AWM Accession No. P06998.01.

Thomas CASEY (30 Jan 1877 - 17 Mar 1956), described as 6' 1 ½" tall, fresh complexion with blue eyes and grey hair, Roman Catholic (*QPF Recruit Register*). Born to John and Francis, Murrough, Ballyvaughan, Clare, Ireland (*Ireland, Civil Registration Births Index, 1864-1958*, Vol 4, p. 281). Sworn into the QPF on 21 Jan 1910, 32yrs, Reg no 1306, Roma Street Station, Brisbane (QSA AF4344). Enlisted with the AIF SERN 3327 on 4 Aug 1915. Embarked with the 24th Australian Infantry Battalion aboard the HMAT *Commonwealth A73* on 26 Nov 1915. Returned to Australia on 8 Nov 1918. Resumed duty on 15 May 1919. Retired 30 January 1937. Died 17 Mar 1956 and buried in plot 7a-130-1 at Toowong Cemetery, Brisbane (QSA AF4344). Honours: 1915 Queensland Police Medal for Merit; 1914/1915 Star; 1919 British War Medal; 1919 Victory Medal.

Claude Edward CASTREE (13 Jul 1892 - 15 Aug 1918 KIA), described as 5' 8" tall, sallow complexion with hazel eyes and brown hair (*QPF Recruit Register*). Born to John and Clara, Blackall, Queensland (*Australia, Birth Index, 1788-1922*-Reg no 000324). Sworn into the QPF on 1 Feb 1913, 20yrs 6mths, Reg no 1700, Townsville Station (QSA AF3137). Enlisted in the AIF on 26 Aug 1915 SERN 2232A. Embarked with the 49th Infantry Battalion aboard HMAT *Armadale* on 18 Sep 1915. Shot and killed at the Somme on 15 Aug 1918 and died at the 13th Australian Field Ambulance Advanced Dressing Station. Buried in the Villers-Bretonneux Military Cemetery, Villers-Bretonneux, Somme, France. Honours: 1914/1915 Star; 1919 British War Medal; 1919 Victory Medal. Photographs: PM5443. Killed in action.

John CHRISTIANSEN (6 Feb 1893 - 22 Nov 1915 KIA), described as 5' 9 ¼" tall, fair complexion with grey eyes and fair hair, Church of Christ (*QPF Recruit Register*). Born to Arthur and Gertrude, Tent Hill, Gatton, Queensland. Sworn into the QPF on 28 Apr 1914, 21yrs 2mths, Reg no 1846, Beenleigh Station (QSA QF2839). Enlisted in AIF on 14 Jan 1915, SERN 1011. Embarked with the 5th Australian Light Horse Regiment on 12 Jun 1915 aboard the HMAT *Karoola A63* for Egypt. Killed in action on the Gallipoli Peninsula, Turkey on 22 Nov 1915. Buried in plot IG2 in the Shell Green Cemetery, Gallipoli Peninsula, Canakkale Province, Turkey. Honours: 1914/1915 Star; 1919 British War Medal; 1919 Victory Medal; Photographs: *The Queenslander Pictorial* supplement to *The Queenslander*, 14 Aug 1915, p. 28 (SLQ Image No 702692-19150814-s0028). Killed in Action.

Bertram George COLE (11 Feb 1884 - 22 Mar 1948), described as 6' 2" tall, ruddy complexion with blue eyes and brown hair, Church of England (*QPF Recruit Register*). Born to George and Mary, Islington, London, England (*England and Wales Birth Index 1837-1915*). Served in South African Police Force 4 Dec 1909 to 31 May 1912. Sworn into the QPF on 6 Nov 1912, 28yrs 9mths, Reg no 1666, Roma Street Station, Brisbane (QSA AF35930). Enlisted in the AIF SERN 6493 on 6 Apr 1915. Embarked with the 7th Australian Infantry Brigade Train, 17th Company Army Service Corps aboard HMAT *Ascanius A11* on 24 May 1915. Sergeant Cole returned to Australia on 23 Jun 1920 (Enlistment paperwork). Resumed duty with the QPF on 23 Sep 1920, 36yrs, Petrie Terrace Police Depot, Brisbane. Resigned 21 Oct 1923. Returned to the United Kingdom and married Kathleen Monica Nolan at St Martin, London in Jun 1931. Returned to Australia in 1946 as Co-Director of Horlicks Slough. Died 22 Mar 1948 in Sydney, New South Wales, his ashes interred in the Northern Suburbs Crematorium ('Family Notices', *The Sydney Morning Herald*, 23 Mar 1948, p. 12). Honours: 1914/1915 Star; 1919 British War Medal; 1919 Victory Medal.

Alexander CRUICKSHANK (23 Jul 1888 - 19 Dec 1963), described as 5' 9 ¼" tall, dark complexion with brown eyes and brown hair, Methodist (*QPF Recruit Register*). Born to Alexander and Annabella, Adelaide, South Australia. Sworn into the QPF on 11 Dec 1913, 24yrs 4mths, Reg no 1794, Fortitude Valley Station, Brisbane (QSA AF3230). Enlisted with the AIF SERN 3027 on 12 Jul 1915. Embarked with the 26th Australian Infantry Battalion aboard HMAT *Itonus A50* on 30 Dec 1915. Returned to Australia on 13 Feb 1917 injured in left forearm and hand (Enlistment paperwork). Resumed QPF duty on 31 May 1917, Petrie Terrace Police Depot, Brisbane. Resigned 31 Jul 1919 (QSA AF3230). Married Rachel Davidson on 21 Jan 1920 (*Australian marriage Index 1788-1949*). Died 19 Dec 1963. Photograph: PM4550.

Archibald John CURVEY (13 June 1886 - 3 May 1917 KIA) described as 5' 8 ¾" tall, ruddy complexion with brown hair and brown eyes, Church of England. Born to William and Elizabeth, Tenterfield, New South Wales (Australia Birth Index, 1788-1922 - Registration Number 34464). Sworn into the QPF on 1 Jul 1910, 24yrs 1mth, Reg no 1346, Winton Station (QSA AF3190). Enlisted in the QIF on 26 Oct 1915 SERN 4675. Embarked with the 20th Battalion on 13 of April 1916 aboard HMAT *Ceramic A40* for England. During April of 1917 the 20th Battalion relieved in and out of the line at outpost positions in front of Lagnicourt and Noreuil. Lance Corporal Curvey was killed in action by a shell, during the Battle of Bullecourt on 3 May 1917 (NAA 3480322). His body was never recovered. Memorialised at the Villers-Bretonneux Memorial, Villers-Bretonneux, Picardie, France. Honours: 1914/1915 Star; Photographs: PM4561. Killed in action.

Thomas DEDMAN (29 Mar 1882 - 26 Jul 1916 KIA) described as 5' 10" tall, fresh complexion with blue eyes and brown hair, Wesleyan (*QPF Recruit Register*). Born to Charles and Elizabeth, Walhalla, Victoria (QSA AF2979). Sworn into the QPF on 1 Oct 1909, 27yrs 6mths, Reg No 1275, Roma Street Station (QSA AF2979). Enlisted in AIF on 21 Jul 1915 SERN 2592, embarked with the 26th Battalion on 21 Oct 1915 aboard HMAT *Seang Bee* A48 for Egypt. Corporal Dedman, 12th Battalion killed in action at Pozieres in France at some point between 23 and 26 Jul 1916. Memorialised on the Villiers Bretonneux Wall of Remembrance, France. Honours: 1914/1915 Star; British War Medal; 1919 Victory Medal; Photographs: PM3888. Killed in action.

Patrick (Joseph) DEVINE (7 Mar 1886 – 3 Nov 1917 KIA) Patrick Devine was born into a large Roman Catholic family on 17 March 1886 in Skeaghvasteen, Kilkenny, Ireland. According to the *Census of Ireland 1901*, he lived with his parents, Patrick (55) and Elizabeth, or Eliza, (50), his grandmother Mary, who was 82 at the time, seven siblings (out of nine) and a young niece, Eliza Lowe (5). Patrick came from a fairly well-educated family. His father was a 'Sub Postmaster' and his mother, originally from Dublin City, worked as the District Midwife. Patrick, 14 years old at the time of the Census, also worked at the Post Office, as a rural postman. The *Census of Ireland 1911* shows that Patrick Devine senior still held the position of the Sub Postmaster while his wife assisted him as the Postmistress. Only five children were now remaining in the family home. On 10 August 1908, Patrick Devine joined the Royal Irish Constabulary (RIC, HO1084, NA UK). There is one record of him serving in Brawney, Athlone, county

Westmeath. On 27 October 1913, he resigned from the RIC to emigrate to Australia.

Only four months after leaving the Irish Constabulary, Patrick Joseph Devine, Reg No 1805, applied to join the Queensland Police Force (QPF). The *Recruit Register* describes Patrick as 5 feet 11 and a quarter inch tall, measuring 37 inches across the chest (QSA AF3127; NAA 3503373), of fresh complexion with blue eyes and dark hair. He was sworn in on 11 February 1914. Candidates with previous service with the Irish Constabulary, any urban police, or any military/law enforcement agencies were actively sought out by the colonial forces.

As Patrick volunteered to enlist into the AIF so soon after joining the QPF, his Queensland Police service record is brief. His spent his short career as a policeman in the Traffic Office at Roma Street Station. An electoral list from February 1915 gives Constable Devine's address as Roma Street Police station (*Brisbane Courier*, 9 Mar 1915, p. 10). Patrick enlisted into the AIF on 25 June 1915. He was single upon joining the Expeditionary Force. Following a competitive exam, he was appointed 2nd Lieutenant on 30 July 1915. On 21 October 1915, Lt Devine embarked on HMAT A48 *Seang Bee* and left Australia for Suez. On 24 July 1916, Lt Devine, 9th Infantry Battalion AIF, was wounded in Pozieres. The proceedings of a medical board indicated that Patrick was suffering from shell shock. The circumstance of the injury specified that, he was 'blown up and unconscious for half an hour. Carried on till next day, then collapsed. Headache, dreams, tremors, reflexes, plus [sic]' (NAA 3503373). Devine was incapacitated for 8 weeks.

On 8 August 1916, Devine was again hospitalised at the 4th London General Hospital (RAMC). A few months later, on 10 October 1916,

Australian Military Offices, London, the Medical Board found that Lt Devine was still suffering from shell shock. Patrick described that he was 'nervous, and insomniac, sleeps badly, dreams, and has no appetite. Pulse 64-74' (NAA 3503373, p. 11). On 19 February 1917, though still suffering from shell shock, Devine was found fit for general duty (pp. 13, 28-9). On 3 November the same year, Patrick was killed in action by 'a bullet through the head'. He died in the field hospital, Belgium.

Eva Mary Devine of 4 Brighton Buildings, Terenure Rd, Dublin, was listed as the next of kin. It seems Patrick and Eva Mary Bethel got married while he was on leave with shell shock, near the end of 1916 in South Dublin (Eva Mary Bethel, Patrick Joseph Devine, 1916, Oct-December registration quarter; Vol 2, p. 541, *Irish Marriages 1845-1958*). Honours: Star, Bravery War Medal, Victory Medal, Memorial Plaque and Scroll, London. Photograph: P. Devine, F Co., *The Queenslander Pictorial*, supplement to *The Queenslander*, 24 Oct 1914, p. 24 (SLQ Image 702692-19141024-s0024-0004); PM0111; Niall Brannigan & John Kirwan, *Kilkenny Families in the Great War* (2012).

Daryl James Gilchrist DODDS (1889 - 25 Sep 1918 KIA), described as 5" 10" tall, fair complexion with hazel eyes and fair hair, Church of England (*QPF Recruit Register*). Born to William and Ada, Holborn, Middlesex, England. Sworn into the QPF on 4 Mar 1910, 21yrs, Reg no 1312, Toowoomba Station (QSA AF3160). Enlisted in AIF 2 Aug 1915 SERN 1175. Embarked with 11th Light Horse Regiment on 4 Oct 1915 about HMAT *Mashobra A47*. Killed in action at Semakh on the shores of Lake Tiberias, Palestine on 25 Sep 1918. Buried in the Haifa War Cemetery, Haifa, Israel. Honours: 'Mentioned in Dispatches' on 4th April 1918 for distinguished conduct during the action at Sheria where he attempted to save a wounded officer while under fire. Honours: 1914/1915 Star; British War Medal. Killed in action.

Stephen Henry DOUGLAS (17 Aug 1884 - 6 Sep 1930), described as tall 5' 9 ¼", dark complexion with blue eyes and brown hair, Roman Catholic (*QPF Recruit Register*). Born to John and Catherine, Ballarat, Victoria, Australia. Sworn into the QPF on 23 Jan 1908, 23yrs, Reg no 1080, Petrie Terrace Police Depot, Brisbane. Resigned 27 Jun 1911. Re-appointed 19 Dec 1911, Roma Street Station, Brisbane (QSA AF3911). Enlisted with the AIF SERN 10057 on 15 Aug 1915. Embarked with the 7th Australian Field Ambulance aboard HMAT *Star of Victoria A16* on 31 Mar 1916. Returned to Australia on 4 Jun 1919 (enlistment paperwork). Resumed duty with the QPF on 14 Aug 1919, 28yrs, Reg no 1530, Roma Street Station, Brisbane. Married Sarah May Killeen on 18 Sep 1919 in Brisbane. Retired on 16 Aug 1928 (QSA AF3911). Died 6 Sep 1930 and buried in plot RC4-009-0042 at the Drayton & Toowoomba Cemetery. Honours: 1914/1915 Star; British War Medal; 1919 Victory medal.

Patrick DOYLE (3 Jul 1887 - unknown), described as 5' 9 ½" tall, fresh complexion with blue eyes and fair hair, Roman Catholic (*QPF Recruit Register*). Born to James and Bridget, Kilkenny, Ireland. Sworn into the QPF on 26 July 1911, 24yrs 2mths, Reg no 1464, South Brisbane Station, Brisbane. Resigned 21 April 1915 (QSA AF2759). Enlisted with the AIF on 24 Apr 1915 but discharged on 31 May 1915, due to chronic lower back pain (NAA 3520993).

Walter William DUMBRELL (Jul 1883 - 19 Apr 1918 KIA) born in July 1883, to David and Jane (neé Blake, from Port Macquarie) Dumbrell in Galston, NSW. The family had six children, George Alfred Stephen,

Ethel Jane, Albert D, Myrtle Jessie Cornelia, Alma Irene Blake and Walter William. The Dumbrells belonged to the Church of England.

In 1899, at 17-years-old Dumbrell volunteered to fight in the Second Boer War. From 1815, the southern point of South Africa was divided between the British colonies and Dutch Afrikaans settlers, the Boers. The latter eventually organised into republics of the Orange Free State and the Transvaal. The first major conflict erupted between the British and the Boers in 1880. Shortly, gold and diamonds were discovered in the republics causing an influx British of subjects in search of wealth. The rising tensions culminated in the Second South African War, 1899-1902. At the onset of the conflict, the Australian colonies supported the war with each colony, sending four to six contingents to bolster the imperial effort.

Dumbrell enlisted with the 5th Queensland Imperial Bushmen Regiment (535) on 10 May 1900. 'Prior to Federation (1901) enlistment was to separate Australian colonial forces. Attestation proformas [were] contained in Conditions of service of South African and over-sea contingents employed in the South African War, 1899-1902' (HMSO, 1904). The first detachment, the 5th Queensland Imperial Bushmen Contingent arrived in Cape Town on 31 March 1901. These men were specially selected for height, with no man above 177 cm or below 167 cm. The soldiers were paid 5 shillings (50¢) per day from date of embarkation plus 1 shilling (10¢) per day extra of 'Colonial Allowance'. Imperial bushmen regiments were paid for by the imperial government in London (Murray, *Official Records of the Australian Military Contingents to the War in South Africa, 1899-1902*).

Dumbrell was a Doyle's Scout, a member of 'a corps of specially selected men, raised by Captain R D Doyle, DSO, of the New South Wales forces. Doyle had served in the 6th Imperial Bushmen and the 3rd Regiment of

New South Wales Bushmen. The officers and men were not, however, restricted to those from New South Wales ('Doyle's Scouts, Australian Units', Anglo-BoerWar.com). As the conflict continued and casualties mounted, the Australians (now federated) became disenchanted with the war. On 27 March 1902, Dumbrell's unit embarked on the *St Andrew* arriving in Brisbane on 30 April 1902, stopping en route in Albany and Melbourne. The unit was disbanded on 5 May 1902 (*The Boer War Memorial*). Over 400,000 soldiers from all around the empire fought on the British side.

Between 1904 and 1909, Dumbrell was employed by Mr Ballerie of Woorooma in general bush and station work, as well as by Mr F Ingram, Book Book Station Wagga, and by the NSW Government on the Barren Jack Water Scheme, the Burrinjuck Dam. 'The Barren Jack Creek Water Supply Dam was built on Barren Jack Creek close to the temporary settlement of Barren Jack City to facilitate supply of water by gravity from the dam to the settlement. (DLWC S170 Register) Dumbrell's last employer before transition into the police work was a shearing contractor Mr W Green of Longreach, QLD.

Dumbrell joined the Queensland Police Force on 2 December 1909 and was sworn in on 4 March 1910. He is described as 6 feet and ¼ inches tall, of fresh complexion with brown eyes and hair; and as a quiet steady man with fair education, who could ride a bicycle but was a very poor horseman (*QPF Register*). Following his three-months-long depot training, Constable Dumbrell was stationed in Rockhampton in March 1910. Late at night on 22 July 1910, he received his first reprimand for gossiping with a female while on duty in Queen Street. He pleaded not guilty to the charge stating he was answering the woman's queries. The witness testimonies by Inspector Toohey and Sergeant Carmony showed Dumbrell was talking to the woman for 5 minutes. He was subsequently found guilty by Commissioner Cahill (Record of conduct and service, Dumbrell, QSA AF3085).

In 1912, Dumbrell was transferred to Banana, QLD and following a short term there he was transferred to Rockhampton in June 1913, now a married man. Having served the minimum required time in the police, Constable Dumbrell married Grace Lilly Evans on 12 May 1913 (Reg No 002888, p. 7136). A year later their son, Walter David Dumbrell, was born on 30 July 1914 (died on 10 Dec 1999, buried at Mount Morgan Cemetery, Rockhampton/ QSA AF3085). In March 1915, the family relocated to Many Peaks station. A half a year later, on 15 September 1915, Constable Dumbrell requested unlimited leave of absence to volunteer for active service with the Australian Expeditionary Forces.

On 18 September 1915, Dumbrell enlisted in the AIF. In the months between enlistment and embarkation for England, Dumbrell's mother passed away. She died on 29 October 1915 of heart disease (Series 2765, Item X2090, Roll 343, State Archives NSW). On 18 June 1916, Dumbrell embarked on HMAT *Demosthenes A64* from Sydney for Plymouth, arriving two months later, on 20 July (NAA 3525470). In November 1916, he left for France with the 41st Battalion, 11th Brigade. At the end of December, he was hospitalised with frontal simisitis [sic] (sinusitis) for a week. Mid-January 1917, Dumbrell re-joined his unit in Rouelles. For the majority of 1917, he remained in the field, receiving promotion initially to Lance Sergeant in June and finally to Sergeant in July 1917.

In September 1917, Dumbrell attended the Lewis Gun School of Musketry, Tidworth, qualifying as 1st class instructor. In November, he was moved to the 9th battalion and proceeded to France from Southhampton.

In March 1918, he was mobilised with the 41st battalion back to Rouelles joining the action on the front. Over the course of a year and a half the 41st Battalion was engaged at Armentieres and Ploegsteert Wood. There Dumbrell was affected badly by gas and had to be carried out of the line. Sgt Dumbrell was killed in shellfire the following month on 19 April 1918 'in the trenches North of the Bray, Corbie Road. Death was instantaneous. He was buried by Chaplin Rev ZZ Mills, MC of this battalion, about 1000 yards north of Sailley-le-Sec, about 3 miles south-west of Morlacourt, France. A suitable cross has been erected' (NAA 3525470).

In 1918, Dumbrell's widow and son were granted military pension of £2 13s 9d and £1 per fortnight respectively. Dumbrell was re-interned in 1923 at Villers-Bretonneux Military Cemetery, Villers-Bretonneux, Departement de la Somme, Picardie, France. Awards: Star, British War Medal, Victory Medal. Photograph: PM3189; AWM Accession No P0 6535.001.

John 'Jack' FITZGERALD (Jan 1892 - 30 Mar 1918 KIA), described as 5' 9" tall, dark complexion with grey eyes and brown hair, Roman Catholic (*QPF Recruit Register*). Born in Allora, Queensland. Sworn into the QPF on 2 Jun 1915, 23yrs 6mths, Reg no 2026, Petrie Terrace Police Depot, Brisbane (*QPF Recruit Register*). Enlisted with the AIF SERN 21218 on 4 Oct 1915. Embarked with the 9th Australian Field Artillery Brigade aboard HMAT *Argyllshire* A8 on 11 May 1916. Killed at dawn on 30 March 1918, at Sailly-Le-Sec, when an enemy shell landed a few yards away, killing him instantly (AWM/Qld Police Memorial). He buried in Heilly Station Cemetery, Mericourt-L'Abbe, Picardie, France. Honours: 1914/1915 Star; British War Medal; 1919 Victory medal. Photographs: PM4551. Killed in action.

Herbert FORREST (Mar 1893 - 12 Oct 1917 KIA), described as 5' 9 ¾" tall, fresh complexion with blue eyes and brown hair, Nonconformist (*QPF Recruit Register*). Born to Albert and Sarah, Middleton, Lancashire, England. Sworn into the QPF on 3 Nov 1914, 21yrs 8mths, Reg no 1948, Fortitude Valley Station, Brisbane. Dismissed 10 May 1915 (QSA AF2771). Enlisted with the AIF SERN 6768 on 21 Sep 1915. Embarked with the 9th Australian Infantry Battalion aboard HMAT *Marathon A74* on 27 Oct 1916. Killed in action as part of the 49th Australian Infantry Battalion in Belgium on 12 Oct 1917. Remembered at the Menin Gate Memorial, Ypres, Flanders, Belgium (NAA 4024320). Honours: British War Medal; 1919 Victory medal. Killed in action.

Frederick GEISE (14 Nov 1880 - 02 Jul 1903), described as 5' 8" tall, fresh complexion with brown hair and brown eyes, Church of England (QPF Register). Born to Ernest and Pauline, Bingera, Gwydir District, New South Wales (Ancestry). Sworn into the QPF 2 Jul 1903, 22yrs 7mths, Reg no 81, Roma Street Station (QSA AF4172). 18 Aug 1908 married Evelyn Lilian Bishop, Milton, Brisbane. Enlisted into the AIF on 27 Aug 1915 SERN 2079. Embarked 7 Sep 1916 with the 41st Australian Infantry Battalion. Returned to Australia 10 May 1919. Re-appointed into the QPF on 25 Jul 1919, Reg no 736, Stables, Petrie Terrace Police Depot (QSA AF4172). Retired 19 Jul 1934 at Townsville. Died on 13 Jun 1951, Brisbane General Hospital. Photographs: AWM Accession No 3802496.

Oswald Horatio GOODRICH (May 1894 - 12 Oct 1917 KIA), described as 6' 2" tall, dark complexion with brown eyes and brown hair, Methodist (*QPF Recruit Register*). Born to Robert and Henrietta, Maclean, New South Wales (*Australia, Birth Index, 1788-1922*, Reg no 23814). Sworn into the QPF on 14 May 1915, 21yrs, Reg no 2014, Roma Street Station (QSA AF3234). Enlisted in the AIF along with three of his brothers on 13 Aug 1915 SERN 3034. Embarked with 47th Battalion aboard *Warilda A69* for Egypt on 5 Oct 1915. Killed by a shell splinter at Passchendaele Ridge, Belgium on 12 Oct 1917. Buried in the Tyne Cot Cemetery, Belgium. Honours: 1914/1915 Star; British War Medal; 1919 Victory medal; Photographs: PM4562. Killed in action.

Robert James HAMILTON (29 Mar 1891 - 27 Jun 1959), described as 5' 9 ½" tall, dark complexion with grey eyes and brown hair, Church of England (*QPF Recruit Register*). Born to Charles and Mary, Humpybong, Queensland. Sworn into the QPF on 30 Sep 1913, 22yrs 6mths, Reg no 1775, Roma Street station, Brisbane (QSA AF3581). Enlisted with the AIF SERN 11 on 17 Apr 1915. Embarked with the 7th Australian Infantry Brigade aboard HMAT *Aeneas A60* on 29 Jun 1915. Returned to Australia on 17 Apr 1920. Re-appointed to the QPF on 5 Aug 1920, Petrie Terrace Police Depot, Brisbane. Resigned on 30 Sep 1923 (QSA AF3581). Died 27 Jun 1959 at Alice Springs, Northern Territory. Honours: 1914/1915 Star; British War Medal; 1919 Victory medal.

William Henry HARTWIG (21 Sep 1891 - 14 Jan 1976), described as 6' tall, fair complexion with blue eyes and fair hair, Church of England (*QPF Recruit Register*). Born to Frank and Annie, Eidsvold, Queensland. Sworn into the QPF on 26 Apr 1912, 19yrs 7mths, Reg no 1582, Petrie Terrace Police Depot, Brisbane. Resigned (QSA AF4691). Enlisted with the AIF SERN 20957 on 23 Nov 1915. Embarked with the 9th Australian Field Artillery Brigade aboard HMAT *Argyllshire A8* on 11 May 1916. Returned to Australia on 11 May 1919. Re-appointed to the QPF on 14 Aug 1919, 25yrs 1mth, Petrie Terrace Police Depot, Brisbane. Married Mabel Eva Bailey on 25 Jul 1925. Retired on 24 Jun 1943 (QSA AF4691). Died 14 Jan 1976 and buried in Eidsvold Cemetery, Queensland. Honours: 1914/1915 Star; British War Medal; 1919 Victory medal.

William John HUGHES (30 May 1884 - 03 May 1915 KIA), described as 5' 9 ½" tall, fresh complexion with blue eyes and fair hair, Presbyterian (*QPF Recruit Register*). Born to William and Susan, Armagh, Altnamachi/ Altnamackan/ Alt na Meacan, Ireland. Nine years' experience as a police officer in the United Kingdom before emigrating to Australia. Sworn into the QPF on 28 Apr 1914, 29yrs 11mths, Reg no 1851, West End Station (QSA AF2784). Enlisted in the AIF SERN 1335 on 13 Jan 1915. Embarked with the 15th Australian Infantry Battalion aboard HMAT *Seang Bee A48* for Egypt on 13 Feb 1915. Killed in action at the Dardanelles, Turkey on 3 May 1915, his body was not recovered. Memorialised at the Lone Pine Memorial, Gallipoli, Turkey. Honours: 1914/1915 Star; British War Medal; 1919 Victory medal. Killed in action.

John JOHNSTON (23 Mar 1888 - 07 May 1915 KIA), described as 5' 9" tall, fresh complexion, blue eyes and brown hair, Presbyterian (*QPF Recruit Register*). Born to John and Annie, Muckross, Kesh, County Fermanagh, Ireland (QSA AF2834). Sworn into the QPF on 22 Dec 1914, 26yrs 9mths, Reg No 1963, Roma Street Station (QSA AF2834). Enlisted in the AIF SERN 1341 on 13 Jan 1915. Embarked with the 15th Australian Infantry Battalion aboard the HMAT *Seang Bee A48* for Egypt on 13 Feb 1915. Killed in action at Gallipoli, Dardanelles, Turkey on 7 May 1915. Buried in the 4th Battalion Parade Ground Cemetery, Gallipoli Peninsula, Canakkale Province, Turkey. Honours: 1914/1915 Star. Killed in action.

Thomas John JUDGE (Aug 1884 - unknown), described as 5' 9" tall, fair complexion with grey eyes and fair hair, Church of England (*QPF Recruit Register*). Born in Wolstanton, Staffordshire, England (*England & Wales, Civil Registration Birth Index, 1837-1915*). Served with the South Lancashire Regiment. Sworn into the QPF on 11 Feb 1914, 29yrs 6mths,

Reg no 1811, West End Station, Brisbane (QSA AF3207). Enlisted as a 2nd Lieutenant with the AIF on 9 Jul 1915 SERN W2584 (NAA 7365779). Embarked with the 31st Australian Infantry Battalion aboard HMAT *Seang Choon A49* on 4 May 1916. Returned to Australia on 15 Feb 1918, but did not resume QPF duty, discharged 8 May 1919 (QSA AF3207). Honours: 1914/1915 Star; British War Medal; 1919 Victory medal.

John Barton KIRKWOOD (May 1885 - 20 Jun 1960), described as 5' 11" tall, fair complexion with hazel eyes and brown hair, Church of England (*QPF Recruit Register*). Born to David and Jeannie, Ashfield, New South Wales. Sworn into the QPF on 26 Jul 1911, 26yrs 2mths, Reg no 1470, South Brisbane Station, Brisbane. Dismissed 4 May 1914 (QSA AF2613). Enlisted with the AIF SERN 2619 on 11 June 1915. Embarked with the 13th Australian Infantry Battalion aboard HMAT *Runic A54* on 9 Aug 1915. Wounded in action 10 Aug 1916, re-joined unit in October. Returned to Australia on 16 Dec 1917. Died 20 Jun 1960 and is memorialised at the Northern Suburbs Memorial Gardens and Crematorium, New South Wales. Honours: 1914/1915 Star; 29.06.1916 DCM; 10.04.1916 Mentioned in Despatches; 1916 British War Medal; 1919 Victory medal.

James KISSANE (1 Apr 1889 – 27 Oct 1957) James Kissane was born on 1 April 1889 in Kilcock Upper, Lissleton, County Kerry, Ireland to parents John Michael and Catherine Cronin (Katie). He came from a large farming Catholic family. James lived with a younger sister, Lizzie, two older sisters, Mary and Norah, and three brothers, Patrick, John and Richard. The farm was quite extensive and contained seven buildings, such as a stable, cow house, calf house, dairy, piggery, a fowl house and a barn. The farmstead also had a servant, Patt Sheehan, aged 26 (*Census Ireland, 1901A*). Kissane departed from London to Brisbane on Oswestry

Grange, Queensland Line, on 18 January 1911 (*UK, Outward Passenger Lists, 1890-1960*).

Supernumerary Kissane was sworn in into the Queensland Police Force on 10 July 1911 (Reg No 1449, QSA 3302). He was 22 years and 3 months at the time. The *QPF* Register, describes James as 5 feel 11 inches tall, with brown eyes and hair, and of fair complexion. His religion is listed as 'Roman Catholic' and previous calling as a 'Labourer' (*Register of Members of the Queensland Police, 1895-1917 and 1879-1924*). 'The majority of recruits were younger sons of farmers, semi-skilled workers and labourers, occupations that implied an unregulated workday. As a rule, the term 'labourer' covered a wide range of employment, predominantly within the unskilled, and often rural, work sector' (Dukova, *A History of the DMP and its Colonial Legacy*, p. 56). Between 1911 and 1915, Constable Kissane received three transfers. He was stationed at Cooyar for nearly a year (1912-1913); Toowoomba for a month (Sept-Oct, 1913); and finally Inglewood. The *Queensland Police Gazette* shows, Kissane made eight arrests with successful convictions in 1915, followed by a custodial sentence for the defendant. The offences ranged from stealing to fraud and obtaining goods or money under false pretences.

On 2 September 1915, aged 26, Kissane volunteered in the Australian Imperial Force. He was soon promoted to the rank of 2nd Lieutenant. He was single, and he listed his brother Patrick as the next of kin. (NAA) Kissane was assigned to 11th Machine Gun Company. He left Australia on 8 June 1916 aboard *HMAT Borda* (A30). In February 1917, he was transferred to the 3rd Division, England. Following a brief period in Pelham Downs, Kissane was taken on strength to 9th Machine Gun Company, attached to 3rd Divisional MGC. On 7 September, he proceeded to France. At the beginning of 1918, he was granted a brief leave to Ireland. On 18 January 1918, Kissane was awarded the Military Cross:

> HIS MAJESTY THE KING has been pleased to confer the undermentioned reward for gallantry and distinguished service in the field.

> For the conspicuous gallantry and devotion to duty when in charge of the company transport establishing a large ammunition dump just behind the forward barrage position. He successfully maintained the supply of ammunition during a critical period despite heavy fire and most difficult condition.

> Extract from the *London Gazette, Fourth and Fifth Supplements*

In March 1918, Kissane was admitted to the General Hospital with a septic right hand. A month later he was invalidated to the United Kingdom. In August, he was re-admitted to hospital with the injury, this time to the Australian Auxiliary Hospital, Harefield Park, Middlesex, England. The No. 1 Australian Auxiliary Hospital was situated at "Harefield Park" in Harefield, Middlesex, and was used as a home for convalescent wounded soldiers of the Australian Imperial Forces (AIF) during the first World War. Following a fortnight at the hospital, Kissane was seconded for duty with Machine Gun Training Depot. Nine months later, he returned to Australia. On 11 October 1919, 2nd Lieutenant's AIF appointment was terminated.

Kissane returned to Brisbane and on 12 September 1919, resumed police duty.

James resigned from the Queensland Police at the end of March 1920, less than a year after getting re-appointed. In 1921, he proceeded to take up a full-time paid position as the Queensland Irish Association (QIA) secretary. He remained in this role until 1924 (*1898-1973 Seventy-Fifth Jubilee of the Queensland Irish Association Souvenir*). At that time, tension between Empire loyalists and Irish nationalists was high and Irish Catholics were under suspicion. Kissane's appointment as secretary would have been strategic: 'it's hard to accuse an Irish Catholic who has won the MC of disloyalty' (special thanks to Dr Rodney Sullivan for this note). The Irish War of Independence was still being waged.

In his official capacity of the secretary of the QIA, Kissane attended a requiem mass for Michael Collins held at St Stephen's Cathedral on 28 August 1922 (*Brisbane Courier*, 29 August 1922, p. 7). Collins was appointed Minister for Finance for Saorstát Eireann during the First Dail Eireann and the chairman of the Provisional Government following the signing of the Anglo-Irish Treaty, 1921. He was assassinated at , County Cork by the Anti-Treatyites on 22 August during the Irish Civil War (also see Dukova, 2016).

James married Mary Agnes O'Driscoll 'according to the rites of the Roman Catholic Church' on 10 July 1922 (1922/B/30439), in 'Dara' on Gotha Street, Valley, Brisbane. 'Dara' housed Archbishop of Brisbane Duhig between 1917 and 1928. Mary Agnes was a daughter of Kate Mary Cecilia Hayes and Andrew O'Driscoll, the Queensland Police Inspector.

In April 1923, former Police Sergeant Michael Daley brought charges of assault against James Kissane. The case was dealt with at the Summons

Court. Daley stated that Kissane pushed him by the arm from the QIA club premises. Kissane's answer was to the effect that Daley was suspended for numerous breaches of club rules (distributing advertisements calling for the end of Tory proposals by the executive) and notified of the said suspicion. Daley claimed he intended to appeal, which was the reason of his return. While in the rooms, Daley indicated he will not leave until Kissane lay a hand on him, which he 'gently' did and walked him out of the rooms. Constable Christie present at the scene testified to the same. The case was dismissed, with the professional and witnesses' costs ruled against the complainant (*The Daily Mail*, 17 Apr 1923, p. 8). Kissane resigned from his role of the secretary in 1924. Upon his resignation from the QIA in 1924, he was presented with a watch for his services (*Brisbane Courier*, 12 January 1925, p. 4). Membership of the QIA numbers peaked in 1925, at 815 members. Only men born in Ireland or male descendants of Irish-born parents were admitted at them time, regardless of confession. The Elizabeth Street premises, Tara House, purchased by the club in 1919 for 11,000, attracted regular popularity and use for a variety of events and function (*QIA Souvenir*).

Kissane went on to work as Insurance Inspector. The family lived in 8 Cordelia Street.

Kissane died at Mater Hospital on 27 October 1953 from complications from cancer and heart failure (1953/B/45993). The obituary indicates he was survived by his children, John Andrew, Katherine Mary, and James Morgan, and grandchildren. Kissane is buried in plot LAWN-2-5 at Hemmant Cemetery, Brisbane. Honours: 1914/1915 Star; Military Cross (*London Gazette*, 18 Jan 1918, p. 959, position 19); British War Medal; 1919 Victory medal. Photographs: *Queenslander Pictorial* supplement to *The Queenslander*, 24 Jun 1916, p. 22 (SLQ Image No 702692-19160624-s0022).

Horace Lalor LIDGARD (14 Feb 1889 - 31 Aug 1962), described as 5' 9 ¼" tall, fresh complexion with hazel eyes and brown hair, Church of England (*QPF Recruit Register*). Born to John and Amelia, Gympie, Queensland. Sworn into the QPF on 17 Aug 1914, 25yrs 6mths, Reg no 1898, Petrie Terrace Police Depot, Brisbane. Dismissed 23 Apr 1915 (QSA AF2764). Enlisted with the AIF SERN 3968 on 28 Oct 1915. Embarked with the 25th Australian Infantry Battalion aboard HMAT *Wandilla A62* on 31 Jan 1916. Wounded in action 14 Aug 1916, court marshalled for striking his superior officer 30 Jun 1917, 9mth sentence with hard labour suspended 21 Aug 1917 upon contracting scabies. Sent back to the front 7 Oct 1917, suffered gas attack on 3 Nov 1917, and transferred back to England. Sent back to the front 1 Apr 1918, court marshalled 3 May 1918 for 3 weeks AWOL and sentenced to 51 days detention. Forfeited 4 days' pay for being AWOL 21 Mar 1919. Returned to Australia on 12 Jun 1919, and discharged medically unfit on 20 Sep 1919 (NAA 8195620). Died 31 Aug 1962. Honours: 1914/1915 Star; British War Medal; 1919 Victory medal.

Archibald MacDONALD (23 Apr 1883 – 18 Jul 1976) is described as 5'10" tall, fresh complexion with blue eyes and light brown hair, and Presbyterian (*QPF Recruit Register*). Born to John and Margaret, Benbecula, Inverness Shire, Scotland. Sworn into the QPF on 1 Nov 1910, 25yrs 6mths, Reg no 1376, Petrie Terrace Police Depot, Brisbane. Resigned 31 Jan 1915 (QSA AF4707). Enlisted with the AIF SERN 1868 on 11 Feb 1915. Embarked with the 9th Infantry Battalion aboard HMAT Star of England A15 on 8 Apr 1915. Returned to Australia on 9 Mar 1919 (NAA 1844561). Re-appointed to the QPF on 1 Aug 1919, Reg no 1376, Roma

Street Station, Brisbane. Retired on 23 Apr 1943 (QSA AF4707). Died 18 July 1976. Honours: 1914/1915 Star; British War Medal; 1919 Victory medal. Photographs: PM4555.

Donald MacDONALD (2 Feb 1889 - unknown), described as 5' 8 ¾" tall, fresh complexion with hazel eyes and brown hair, Roman Catholic (*QPF Recruit Register*). Born in Stanthorpe, Queensland. Sworn into the QPF on 26 Jul 1911, 22yrs 6mths, Reg no 1471, Petrie Terrace Police Depot, Brisbane (QSA AF5295). Enlisted with the AIF SERN 2652 on 21 July 1915. Embarked with the 26th Australian Infantry Battalion aboard HMAT *Seang Bee A48* on 21 Oct 1915. Returned to Australia on 12 May 1919 (NAA 1844626). Re-appointed to the QPF on 14 Aug 1919, Roma Street Station, Brisbane. Retired on 2 Feb 1949 (QSA AF5295). Died 15 December 1965. Honours: 1914/1915 Star; British War Medal; 1919 Victory medal; 1919 Mentioned in Despatches.

William Michael Gregory MALOY (13 Jul 1888 – 05 Aug 1955), described as 5' 11 ¼" tall, ruddy complexion with blue eyes and brown hair, Roman Catholic (*QPF Recruit Register*). Born to James and Elizabeth, Lithgow, New South Wales. Sworn into the QPF on 1 Oct 1914, 26yrs 2mths, Reg no 1922, Petrie Terrace Police Depot, Brisbane. Dismissed 29 Dec 1914 (QSA AF 2709). Enlisted with the AIF SERN 1520 on 1 Jan 1915. Embarked with the 15th Australian Infantry Battalion aboard HMAT *Seang Choon A49* on 13 Feb 1915. Court-martialled 26 Mar 1917 for a variety of offences, found guilty and sentenced to 90 days confinement and forfeited £53 in wages. Returned to Australia on 13 Jan 1918 and discharged medically unfit on 27 Jun 1918. Went on to serve during WW2 (NAA 8212696). Died 5 Aug 1955 in Goulburn, New South Wales. Honours: 1914/1915 Star; British War Medal; 1919 Victory medal.

Albert MANSBRIDGE (29 May 1882 - 20 May 1970), described as 5' 11" tall, fair complexion with grey eyes and fair hair, Church of England (*QPF Recruit Register*). Born to William and Tamar, Warrnambool, Victoria. Sworn into the QPF on 13 Feb 1907, 24yrs 10mths, Reg no 965, Petrie Terrace Police Depot, Brisbane. Enlisted with the AIF SERN 6462 on 1 Mar 1915. Embarked with the 17th Australian Company Army Service Corps aboard HMAT Ascanius A11 on 24 May 1915. Returned to Australia on 1 Feb 1918. Discharged on 1 Feb 1918 medically unfit, suffering from gastritis and haemorrhoids. Re-appointed to the QPF on 23 Sep 1918, 36 yeas 4mths, Petrie Terrace Police Depot, Brisbane. Retired on 1 Jun 1921 (QSA AF4302). Died 20 May 1970 and buried in plot CE-24-012 at Warrnambool Cemetery, Victoria. Honours: 1914/1915 Star; British War Medal; 1919 Victory medal.

William Ernest MATTHEWS (Jan 1888 – 14 Jul 1970) described as 5'9" tall, fresh complexion with grey eyes and brown hair, Methodist (*QPF Recruit Register*). Born to William and Mary, Forge Creek, Barnsdale, Victoria. Sworn into the QPF on 3 March 1914, 26yrs 3mths, Reg no 1828, Petrie Terrace Police Depot, Brisbane (QSA AF3447). Enlisted with the AIF SERN 5124 on 17 July 1915. Embarked with the 9th Australian Infantry Battalion aboard HMAT *Star of Victoria A16* on 31 Mar 1916. Suffered shellshock in France on 3 Sep 1916. Returned to Australia on 13 Feb 1917. Re-appointed to the QPF on 31 May 1917, 29yrs 5mths, Roma Street Station, Brisbane. Discharged from the AIF on 6 Jun 1917. Resigned from the QPF on 21 January 1922 (QSA AF3447). Died 14 July 1970 and is memorialised at the Mount Thompson Memorial Gardens and Crematorium, Holland Park West, Brisbane. Honours: 1914/1915 Star; British War Medal; 1919 Victory medal.

Thomas McGILLYCUDDY (Jun 1891 - 08 Jul 1918 KIA) Thomas McGillycuddy, the youngest of five children, was born in 1891 in small townland of Carhoobeg, County Kerry, Ireland to Irish and English-speaking parents, Margaret and Timothy (*Ireland, Civil Registration Births Index, 1864-1958, Vol 5*, p. 257). The McGillycuddies were a Roman Catholic family and lived on a farm stead, which in addition to the main house had a stable, cow and calf houses, a dairy, a piggery and a barn. At 19 Thomas was living in his parents' three-room house in Carhoobeg. He worked on the family farm. (*Census of Ireland, 1911*).

In March 1913, Thomas arrived in Sydney on Westralia (*Unassisted Immigrant Passenger Lists, NSW, 1826-1922*). A few months later he applied to join the Queensland Police Force. On 30 September 1913, Supernumerary McGillycuddy, described as 5 feet and 9 inches tall, of ruddy complexion with brown hair and brown eyes, was sworn in into the Queensland Police Force (Reg No 1784). In October 1914, Constable McGillycuddy was transferred to Bundaberg (*Register of Members of the Queensland Police, 1895-1917 and 1879-1924*).

In August 1915, after barely two years in the service, McGillycuddy enlisted with the Australian Imperial Force, 45th Battalion (initially 47th) SERN 2770. Aged 24, he embarked on HMT Minnewaska and left for Gallipoli (NAA B2455). Thomas was one of few ANZACZs to have survived the disastrous campaign; 7818 men were killed in Turkey in 1915. On Christmas Day 1915, he disembarked as an ex-Anzac at Alexandria. Three months later, he was taken on strength of 47th Battalion, AIF. In June 1916, McGillycuddy proceeded to join the British Expeditionary Forces, arriving in Marseille on *Caledonia* later that month. Throughout 1916-17, Thomas sustained several serious injuries on the Western Front. In August 1916, he was severely wounded in action by a shrapnel in his left hip and right foot and had to be transferred to Dublin for treatment. In September, Thomas was discharged to duty from the Central Military Hospital in Cork, then to the AIF Command Depot No 1, Perham Downs, UK. The next day he was granted a furlough for a fortnight.

In mid-1917, McGillycuddy was back in France where he was shot again and wounded in the left arm. Having passed through the casualty station, Thomas was eventually admitted to General Hospital in Rouen, Normandy, France. In October 1917, upon his release from the hospital he joined a Depot at Le Havre, Normandy. There, he was charged with being out of bounds in a town without a pass (NAA B2455). He was sentenced to 14 days Field Punishment No 2 by the Commanding Officer for the offence. A court-martial, or a commanding officer, awarded field punishment for any offence committed on active service, and could sentence an offender for a period not exceeding, in the case of a court-martial three months, and in the case of a commanding officer 28 days to either Field Punishment No 1 or No 2. Field punishment No. 1 consisted of heavy labouring duties, being restrained in handcuffs or fetters, and being tied to a post or wheel. Field punishment No. 2 differed, in that the offender was not liable to be attached to a fixed object.

> He returned to the front on 14th November [1917] at Peronne where the Battalion was being held in reserve. Next came two stints holding the line at Hollebeke before he was granted two weeks leave. On his return, the 47th Battalion was disbanded due to the depletion of the Battalion as a fighting unit because of the casualties. McGillicuddy was absorbed into the 45th Battalion and detached to the 12th Light Trench Mortar Battery.

Paul Ruge, *Their Glory Shall not be Blotted Out*, 2006.

McGillycuddy was granted a month-long leave to the UK, between March and April 1918. In May, he was taken on strength with the 45th Battalion in France. Six weeks later, Thomas McGillycuddy was killed in action during the Battle of Hamel, just four months and three days before the Armistice. He is buried at Villers-Bretonneux, Departement de la Somme, Picardie, France. Honours: 1914/1915 Star; British War Medal.

Wallace Charles McGILLIVRAY (May 1883 - 18 Jun 1972), described as 5'11½" tall, dark complexion with brown eyes and brown hair, Roman Catholic (*QPF Recruit Register*). Born to Alexander and Margaret, Melbourne, Victoria. Sworn into the QPF on 29 Jan 1912, 28yrs 8mths, Reg no 1559, Petrie Terrace Police Depot, Brisbane. Married Mary Elizabeth Moore on 19 Apr 1915 (*The Queenslander*, 29 May 1915, p. 6). Resigned 30 Apr 1915 (QSA AF3680). Per his QP file, Wallace stated he enlisted with the AIF on 13 January 1915, at Enoggera. Prior to embarking with the Light Horse Regiment, A Squad, D Troop, he was vaccinated for typhoid and smallpox. The company left aboard SS *Medic* on 2 June 1915, but upon reaching Adelaide he was taken ill with rheumatic fever and was sent to hospital there for 2 weeks. Subsequently sent back to hospital at Enoggera. Found unfit for service with sciatica and rheumatism and transferred into the Home Service Reserve Forces and waited until he was called upon. Went home to Esk, and suffered another bout of rheumatic fever, then re-joined QPF 14 Mar 1917 (QSA AF3680; List of officers who have served in the BEF, or AIF in Appx 1). Re-appointed to the QPF on 14 Mar 1917, Reg no 2245, Roma Street Station, Brisbane. Retired on 19 Nov 1924 (QSA AF3680). Died on 18 Jun 1972, and buried in plot E01256 at Esk Cemetery, Queensland.

George McRITCHIE (Nov 1891 - 29 Jul 1916 KIA), described as 5' 8½" tall, fresh complexion with grey eyes and brown hair, Presbyterian (*QPF Recruit Register*). Born to Colin and Sarah, Inverness, Scotland. Sworn into the QPF on 1 Aug 1914, 22yrs 9mths, Reg no 1891, Fortitude Valley Station, Brisbane. Dismissed 8 Dec 1914 (QSA AF2700). Enlisted with the AIF SERN 175 on 12 Jan 1915. Embarked with the 25th Australian Infantry Battalion aboard HMAT *Aeneas* A60 on 29 Jun 1915 (NAA 1959981). Sergeant McRitchie was killed in action at the Battle of the Somme on 29 July 1916 and is memorialised at the Villers-Bretonneux Memorial Cemetery, Villers-Bretonneux, Picardie, France. Honours: 1914/1915 Star; British War Medal; 1919 Victory medal. Killed in action.

Patrick Joseph MORAHAN (06 Feb 1887 – 07 Feb 1971), described as 5' 11 ¼" tall, fair complexion with blue eyes and fair hair, Roman Catholic (*QPF Recruit Register*). Born to Thomas and Winifred in Parish of Clough, Kilkenny. Sworn into the QPF on 4 Jul 1913, 26yrs 5mths, Reg no 1747, Roma Street Station, Brisbane (QSA AF5045). Enlisted with the AIF SERN 544 on 17 May 1915. Embarked with the 26th Australian Infantry Battalion aboard HMAT *Ascanius A11* on 24 May 1915. Wounded in Pozieres and spent three months in hospital in London and wounded again at Bullecourt and spent another 4 months in a Bristol Hospital before returning to the front. Returned to Australia 9 March 1919. Re-appointed to the QPF on 26 May 1919, 33yrs 3mths, Criminal Investigation Branch, Brisbane. Married Phyllis Catherine Laurin on 14 Apr 1920 (*Daily Standard*, 28 Apr 1917, p. 12). Retired on (QSA AF5045). Died 07 Feb 1971 and buried in plot 7A-150-13 at the Toowong Cemetery, Brisbane. Honours: 1914/1915 Star; British War Medal; 1919 Victory medal; Photographs: *Daily Standard*, 28 Apr 1917, p. 12.

Joseph Clifford MORRIS (1894 - 09 Oct 1969), described as 6' 1" tall, dark complexion with brown eyes and brown hair, Church of England (*QPF Recruit Register*). Born to William and Agnes, Barraba, New South Wales. Sworn into the QPF on 15 Feb 1915, 21yrs 2mths, Reg no 1984, Petrie Terrace Police Depot, Brisbane. Enlisted with the AIF SERN 2138 on 21 Jul 1915. Embarked with the 26th Australian Infantry Battalion aboard HMAT *Armadale A26* on 20 Sept 1915. Returned to Australia on 8 Oct 1919. Resigned from the QPF on 10 Oct 1919 (QSA AF3251). Died 9 Oct 1969 and buried in plot A-3 at Rookwood Cemetery, Sydney. Honours: 1914/1915 Star medal; British War Medal; 1919 Victory medal.

Peter MULVIE (22 Nov 1887 - 01 Feb 1917 KIA), described as 5' 9" tall, fresh complexion with hazel eyes and brown hair, Roman Catholic (*QPF Recruit Register*). Born to Thomas and Jessie, Argyle, Scotland. Served with the Glasgow City Police from 21 Oct 1907 to 12 Feb 1912. Sworn into the QPF on 10 Oct 1912, 24yrs 11mths, Reg no 1652, Roma Street Station (QSA AF2966). Enlisted in the AIF SERN 1369 on 13 Jan 1915 (NAA 7986000). Embarked with the 15th Infantry Battalion on 13 Feb 1915 aboard HMAT *Seang Bee A48*. Wounded in action and hospitalised on 8 Aug 1915 and 7 Aug 1916. Killed in action in France on 1 Feb 1917. His body was not recovered. Memorialised at Villers-Bretonneux Memorial, Villers-Bretonneux, Picardie, France. Killed in action. Photographs: PM4563.

James NICHOL (26 Apr 1894 - 4 Nov 1955), described as 6' 2 ¼" tall, fresh complexion with brown eyes and brown hair, Church of England (*QPF Recruit Register*). Born to George and Frances, Maryborough Queensland. Brother to William George. Sworn into the QPF on 8 Jun 1914, 20yrs 1mth, Reg no 1870, Roma Street Station, Brisbane (QSA AF6044). Enlisted with the AIF SERN 9483 on 2 Oct 1915. Embarked with the 2nd Australian Light Horse Field Ambulance aboard HMAT *Commonwealth A73* on 28 March 1916. Returned to Australia on 3 Oct 1919. Resumed duty with the QPF on 9 Oct 1919, Roma Street Station, Brisbane. Retired on 26 Apr 1954 (QSA AF6044). Died 4 Nov 1955 and buried in plot 8-424 at Balmoral Cemetery, Brisbane. Honours: 1914/1915 Star; British War Medal; 1919 Victory medal. Photographs: *The Queenslander Pictorial*, supplement to *The Queenslander*, 18 Mar 1916, p. 23 (SLQ Image No 702692-19160318-s0023-042) *and Truth (Brisbane)*, 21 Apr 1929, p. 14.

William George NICHOL (24 May 1888 - 25 Sep 1964), described as 5' 11 ¼" tall, fresh complexion with brown eyes and brown hair, Church of England (*QPF Recruit Register*). Born to George and Frances, Queensland. Brother to James. Sworn into the QPF on 28 Apr 1914, 25yrs 11mths, Reg no 1857, Petrie Terrace Police Depot Stables, Brisbane (QSA AF4479). Enlisted with the AIF SERN 8913 on 1 Sep 1915. Embarked with the 1st Australian General Hospital aboard HMAT *Ballarat A70* on 16 Feb 1916. Returned to Australia on 15 May 1919. Resumed duty with the QPF on 28 Aug 1919, Petrie Terrace Police Depot, Brisbane. Retired on 10 Aug 1939 (QSA AF4479). Died 25 Sep 1964. Honours: 1914/1915 Star; British War Medal; 1919 Victory medal. Photographs: *The Queenslander Pictorial*, supplement to *The Queenslander*, 01 Apr 1916, p. 27 (SLQ Image No 702692-19160401-s0027-041).

Norman Albert NIELSEN (Jun 1889 – 16 Aug 1970), described as 5' 9 ¾" tall, fair complexion with blue eyes and fair hair, Church of England (*QPF Recruit Register*). Born to Jens and Sarah, Laidley, Queensland. Sworn into the QPF on 17 Jul 1914, 25yrs 1mth, Reg no 1900, Petrie Terrace Police Depot Stables, Brisbane. Dismissed 3 Dec 1915 (QSA AF2833). Enlisted with the AIF SERN 1703 on 9 Dec 1915. Embarked with the

47th Australian Infantry battalion aboard HMT *Hawkes Bay* on 20 April 1916. Invalided back to Australian on 2 Sep 1916. Embarked SERN 2682 with the 41st Infantry Battalion aboard HMAT *Kyarra A55* on 17 Nov 1916. Returned to Australia on 28 Nov 1918 (NAA 7991147). Died 16 Aug 1970 and buried in plot 279 at the Polson Cemetery, Hervey Bay. Honours: 1917 Military Medal; 1914/1915 Star; British War Medal; 1919 Victory medal.

Eugene NUGENT (23 May 1892 - 15 Oct 1915 KIA), described as 5' 9 ¾" tall, fresh complexion with blue eyes and brown hair, Roman Catholic. Born to O? and Annie, Ipswich, Queensland (*QPF Recruit Register*). Sworn into the QPF on 30 Sep 1913, Reg no 1785, 21yrs 4mths, Stables, Petrie Terrace Police Depot (QSA AF2828). Enlisted in the AIF SERN 1723 on 2 Jun 1915. Embarked with the 25thnAustralian Infantry Battalion aboard HMAT *Shropshire A9* on 20 Aug 1915. Killed in Action 15 Oct 1915 at the Dardanelles by a 'bomb fragment wound to forehead' just three days after arrival at front line. Buried in the Embarkation Pier Cemetery at North Beach, Gallipoli. Honours: 1914/1915 Star; Photographs: *The Queenslander Pictorial*, supplement to *The Queenslander*, 14 Aug 1915, p. 22 (SLQ Image No 702692-19150814-s0022-031). Killed in action.

Patrick OLLIVER (12 Jul 1891 - 1975), described as 5' 11 ¾" tall, freckled complexion with hazel eyes and fair hair, Roman Catholic (*QPF Recruit Register*). Born to John and Ellen, Rosewood, Queensland. Sworn into the QPF on 16 Mar 1911, 19yrs 8mths, Reg no 1416, Petrie Terrace Police Depot, Brisbane. Resigned 2 Dec 1914 (QSA AF2695). Enlisted with the AIF SERN 6 on 26 Nov 1915. Embarked with the 14th Australian Light Horse Regiment aboard HMAT *Beltana A72* on 13 May 1916. Suffered mumps on arrival in the UK in Jul 1916, spent 76 days in Hulford Hospital with a venereal disease from 1 Sept 1916, accidentally injured his face in

March 1917, accidentally injured his testes in Aug and then was admitted to the 76th Field Ambulance with scabies in May 1917. Wounded in action, suffered gassing and shell wound on 18 Mar 1918. Suffered from influenza between June and Dec 1918 and then pleurisy from Dec until his return to Australia on 4 Aug 1919 (NAA 7996594). Died in 1975. Honours: 1914/1915 Star; British War Medal; 1919 Victory medal.

Arthur Charles PETERS (Mar 1894 - 15 Oct 1965), described as 5' 8 ¼" tall, fresh complexion with brown eyes and brown hair, Church of England (*QPF Recruit Register*). Born in Walworth, London, England. Sworn into the QPF on 2 Jul 1912, 18yrs 4mths, Reg no 1616, Petrie Terrace Police Depot, Brisbane (QSA AF3150). Enlisted with the AIF SERN 561 on 6 Sep 1915. Embarked with the 41st Australian Infantry Battalion aboard HMAT *Demosthenes A64* on 18 May 1916. Gassed in action in France 14 Oct 1917. Returned to Australia for discharge suffering from tuberculosis of larynx on 12 May 1918. Re-appointed to the QPF on 21 Oct 1918, Petrie Terrace Police Depot, Brisbane. Resigned on 12 Dec 1918 (QSA AF3150). Died 15 Oct 1965 and buried in a Wellington Cemetery, New Zealand. Honours: 1914/1915 Star; 1919 British War Medal; 1919 Victory medal.

Wesley PETERS (16 Mar 1893 - 25 Sep 1968), described as 5' 10 ½" tall, dark complexion with brown eyes and brown hair, Church of England (*QPF Recruit Register*). Born to George and Hanna, Esk, Queensland. Sworn into the QPF on 10 Mar 1913, 20yrs, Reg no 1720, New Farm Station, Brisbane (QSA AF5858). Enlisted with the AIF SERN 2190 on 24 Jun 1915. Embarked with the 25th Australian Infantry Battalion aboard HMAT *Armadale A26* on 18 Sep 1915. Married Constance Sybil Dunn at Nottingham, England on 24 Jun 1919, while on leave. Suffered a gunshot wound to the head on 2 Sep 1918, and was returned to Australia on 9

Dec 1919. Re-appointed to the QPF on 20 Feb 1920, Petrie Terrace Police Depot, Brisbane. Retired on 16 Mar 1953 (QSA AF5858). Died 25 Sep 1958. Honours: 1914 Police Medal for Merit; 1914/1915 Star; British War Medal; 1919 Victory medal.

Edward Henry Randall PHELPS (21 Jan 1891 - 15 Sep 1971), described as 5' 8 ¼" tall, dark complexion with brown eyes and brown hair, Roman Catholic (*QPF Recruit Register*). Born to Henry and Mary, Malbon, Cloncurry. Sworn into the QPF on 13 Mar 1911, 21yrs 2mths, Reg no 1418, Petrie Terrace Police Depot Stables, Brisbane (QSA AF3249). Enlisted with the AIF SERN 2650 on 19 Feb 1915, and embarked with the 4th Australian Light Horse Field Ambulance. Returned to Australia on 28 Feb 1919. Resigned 26 Sep 1919 (QSA AF AF3249). Died 15 Sep 1971 and buried in a Caboolture Cemetery. Honours: 1914/1915 Star; British War Medal; 1919 Victory medal.

Humphrey William PLAYER (24 Jun 1894 - 11 Sep 1970), described as 5' 10 ½" tall, fresh complexion with brown eyes and brown hair, Church of England (*QPF Recruit Register*). Born to Edward and Elizabeth, Angaston, South Australia. Sworn into the QPF on 2 Jun 1915, 20yrs 11mths, Reg no 2032, Roma Street Station, Brisbane (QSA AF3117). Enlisted with the AIF SERN 21396 on 8 Sep 1915. Embarked with the 9th Australian Field Artillery Brigade aboard HMAT *Argyllshire A8* on 11 May 1916. Returned to Australia on 30 Jan 1918. Resigned from the QPF on 16 Sep 1918 (QSA AF3117). Died 11 Sep 1970, and buried in Brighton Cemetery, Holdfast Bay City, South Australia. Honours: 1914/1915 Star; British War Medal; 1919 Victory medal.

Edwin Martin RILEY (10 Jul 1893 – 1967), described as 5' 10 ¼" tall, dark complexion with brown eyes and brown hair, Church of England

(*QPF Recruit Register*). Born to Edwin and Maria, Cooktown, Queensland. Sworn into the QPF on 30 Sep 1913, 21yrs 2mths, Reg no 1788, Fortitude Valley Station, Brisbane. Resigned (QSA AF5374). Enlisted with the AIF SERN 4759 on 20 Sep 1915. Embarked with the 25th Australian Infantry Battalion aboard RMS *Mooltan* on 12 Apr 1916. Wounded in action on 14 Nov 1916. Returned to Australia on 21 Dec 1917. Resumed QPF duty on 21 Mar 1918, Petrie Terrace Police Depot, Brisbane. Retired on 29 Jul 1949 (QSA AF5374). Died 1967 and buried in the Tweed Heads Cemetery, New South Wales. Honours: 1914/1915 Star; British War Medal; 1919 Victory medal; Photographs: *The Queenslander Pictorial*, supplement to *The Queenslander*, 06 Oct 1917, p. 27 (SLQ Image No 702692-19171006-s0027-0041).

Robert Nelson RITCHIE (Jul 1883 - 19 Jul 1915 KIA), described as 5' 10" tall, fair complexion with blue eyes and fair hair, Presbyterian (*QPF Recruit Register*). Born to David and Ann, Tumbulgum, New South Wales. Sworn into the QPF on 10 Mar 1915, 21yrs 9mths, Reg no 1997, South Brisbane Station (QP AF2840). Enlisted in the AIF SERN 1568 on 3 Apr 1915. Embarked with the 25th Australian Infantry Battalion aboard the HMAT *Aeneas A60* on 29 Jun 1915. On 19 Jul 1915, died of illness at sea on his way to the Western front and was buried at sea. Honours: 1914/1915 Star; Photographs: *The Queenslander Pictorial*, supplement to *The Queenslander*, 25 Sep 1915, p. 28 (SLQ Image No 702692-19150925-s0028-032). Killed in action.

Albert Victor ROBERTS (18 Sep 1889 - 4 Jul 1916), described as 5' 11 ¼" tall, fair complexion with blue eyes and fair hair, Lutheran (*QPF Recruit Register*). Born to Charles and Augusta, Gympie, Queensland. Sworn into the QPF on 6 Oct 1911, 22yrs 1mth, Reg no 1502, Petrie Terrace Police Depot, Brisbane. Married Ada Victoria Allan on 24 Feb

1915. Discharged from the QPF for marrying without consent on 20 Mar 1915 (QSA AF2741). Enlisted with the AIF SERN 1991 on 25 Jun 1915. Embarked with the 25th Australian Infantry Battalion aboard HMAT *Kyarra A55* on 16 Aug 1915. Died of wounds 4 Jul 1916, and buried in Bailleul Communal Cemetery Extension (Nord), Lille, Nord Pas de Calais, France, (NAA 8032914). Honours: 1914/1915 Star; British War Medal; 1919 Victory medal.

Joseph Friedrich RUHLE (29 Jan 1891 - 21 Aug 1945), described as 5' 11" tall, dark complexion with blue eyes and brown hair, Roman Catholic (*QPF Recruit Register*). Born to Joseph and Sophia, Townsville, Queensland. Sworn into the QPF on 3 Mar 1914, 23yrs 1mth, Reg no 1831, Roma Street Station, Brisbane, Brisbane (QSA AF4521). Enlisted with the AIF SERN 5180 on 11 Oct 1915. Embarked with the 49th Australian Battalion aboard HMAT *Star of Victoria A16* on 31 Jun 1916. Suffered shell wounds to right arm and chest on 16 Aug 1918. Returned to Australia on 12 Dec 1918. Resumed QPF duty on 10 Apr 1919, Petrie Terrace Police Depot, Brisbane. 27 Feb 1924 married Jane Maddock then widowed on 15 Dec 1924. Remarried Maude Mary Schalk on 15 Oct 1927. Retired on 7 May 1940 (QSA AF4521). Died 21 Aug 1945 in Brisbane. Honours: 1914/1915 Star; British War Medal; 1919 Victory medal.

Timothy SHANNON (Feb 1889 - unknown), described as 5' 8" tall, fresh complexion with blue eyes and brown hair, Roman Catholic (*QPF Recruit Register*). Born to Michael and ?, Thomastown, Kilkenny, Ireland. Served with the Royal Irish Constabulary for six years. Sworn into the QPF on 24 Aug 1914, 25yrs 6mths, Reg no 1908, Petrie Terrace Police Depot Stables, Brisbane. Resigned 30 Nov 1915 (QSA AF2831). Enlisted with the AIF SERN 342 on 28 Dec 1915 with the 41st Australian Infantry Battalion.

Charged with being illegally absent from the AIF Depot from 11 Aug 1916 to 21 Jul 1920, discharged 21 July 1920 (NAA 8080028).

Edwin Alfred SHEPHERD (26 May 1884 - 17 Sep 1954), described as 5' 9 ½" tall, fresh complexion with grey eyes and black hair, Church of England (*QPF Recruit Register*). Born to Frederick and Rosa, Warminster, Wiltshire, England. Sworn into the QPF on 6 Apr 1909, 25yrs, Reg no 1226, Petrie Terrace Police Depot, Brisbane (QSA AF3298). Applied for a Commission in AIF as 2nd Lieutenant on 30 Aug 1915. Embarked with the 26th Australian Infantry Battalion aboard HMAT *Warilda* on 5 Oct 1915. Returned to Australia on 1 Nov 1919. AIF appointment terminated at Brisbane on 15 Feb 1920 (NAA 8081717). Resigned from the QPF on 22 Mar 1920 (QSA AF3298). Honours: 1914/1915 Star; British War Medal; 1919 Victory medal.

Henry Frederick SHEPHERD (21 Jun 1879 - 1964), described as 6' ¾" tall, fair complexion with blue eyes and brown hair, Church of England (*QPF Recruit Register*). Born to Frederick and Rosa, Warminster, Wiltshire, England. Brother to Edwin Alfred Shepherd. Served for one year in the Boer War. Sworn into the QPF on 6 Apr 1909, 30yrs, Reg no 1227, Petrie Terrace Police Depot, Brisbane (QSA AF3304). Enlisted with the AIF SERN 4053 on 31 August 1915. Embarked with the 25th Australian Infantry Battalion aboard HMAT *Commonwealth A73* on 28 March 1916. Returned to Australia on 5 Jan 1920. Discharged from the QPF on 7 Apr 1920 (QSA AF3304). Honours: 1914/1915 Star; British War Medal; 1919 Victory medal.

Frederick Norman Joseph SPENCER (21 May 1894 - 22 Mar 1942), described as 6' 3" tall, sallow complexion with blue eyes and brown hair, Church of England (*QPF Recruit Register*). Born to John and Harriet,

Avondale, Queensland. Sworn into the QPF on 1 Oct 1914, 20yrs 4mths, Reg no 1928, Roma Street Station, Brisbane (QSA AF4095). Enlisted with the AIF SERN 1672 on 8 Jul 1915. Embarked with the 31st Australian Battalion aboard HMAT *Kyarra A55* on 3 Jan 1916. Suffered a gunshot wound to his right shoulder on 19 Oct 1917. Lance Corporal Spencer proceeded back to the front on 20 Mar 1918, but suffered a serious bout of pleurisy in France and was invalided back to Australia on 4 Jan 1919. Re-appointed to the QPF on 28 Sep 1919, Petrie Terrace Police Depot, Brisbane. Retired on 14 Jan 1933 (QSA AF4095). Died 22 Mar 1942 and buried in plot 4-65-44 in the Lutwyche Cemetery, Brisbane. Honours: 1914/1915 Star; British War Medal; 1919 Victory medal. Photographs: *Queenslanders who fought in the Great War*, p. 242 (SLQ Image No 704259-s0242-0002).

Charles Arthur SUTTON (29 Mar 1890 - 20 Jun 1918 KIA), described as 5' 8 ½" tall, dark complexion with brown eyes and black hair, Church of England (*QPF Recruit Register*). Born to Charles and Adeline, Queensland. Sworn into the QPF on 22 Nov 1911, 21yrs 8mths, Reg no 1527, Roma Street Station, Brisbane. Resigned 9 Mar 1914. After resigning Charles took up farming in Gayndah and married Julia Agnes in Jun 1915 (QSA AF2584). Enlisted with the AIF SERN 2903 on 14 Jun 1915. Embarked with the 9th Australian Infantry Battalion aboard HMAT *Ayrshire A33* on 1 Sep 1915. Killed in action near Albert in France on 20 Jun 1918. Memorialised at Villers-Bretonneux, Departement de la Somme, Picardie, France. Honours: 1914/1915 Star; British War Medal; 1919 Victory medal. Killed in action.

Joseph Sylvester Vinson THOMPSON (Jan 1885 - 25 Jul 1916 KIA), described as 5' 8" tall, ruddy complexion with brown and fair hair, Wesleyan (*QPF Recruit Register*). Born to Henry and Margaret, Barraba,

New South Wales (*Australia Birth Index, 1788-1922* - Reg no 33085). Sworn into the QPF on 24 Mar 1908, 23yrs 3mths, Reg no 1130, Roma Street Station (QSA AF2912). Enlisted in the AIF SERN 2883 on 9 Jul 1915. Embarked with the 25th Australian Infantry Battalion aboard HMAT *Seang Bee A48* on 21 Oct 1915 (NAA 834667). Corporal Thompson was killed in action at Pozieres on 25 Jul 1916. Memorialised in the Villers-Bretonneux Memorial, Villers-Bretonneux, Picardie, France. Honours: 1914/1915 Star; Photographs: *The Queenslander Pictorial*, supplement to *The Queenslander*, 22 Jan 1916, p. 22 (SLQ Image No 702692-19150814-s0023-0052). Killed in action.

Harold George **WALKER** (1 May 1896 - 1972), described as 6' ¼" tall, fresh complexion with brown eyes and brown hair, Church of England (*QPF Recruit Register*). Born to Walter and Jane, Toowoomba, Queensland. Sworn into the QPF on 31 Mar 1915, 18yrs 11mths, Reg no 2013, Petrie Terrace Police Depot, Brisbane. Dismissed 25 Jun 1915 (QSA AF2781). Enlisted with the AIF SERN 1277 on 7 Jul 1915. Embarked with the 5th Australian Light Horse Regiment aboard HMAT *Hymettus A1* on 17 Dep 1915. Wounded by gunshot to right leg on 31 Jul 1917. In late 1918, Harold was fined for being AWOL, neglecting to obey orders, conduct to the prejudice of good order and military discipline and for ill-treating a horse, for which he received time in military prison. Returned to Australia on 10 Jun 1919 and discharged on 6 Oct 1919 (NAA 3004604). Died in 1972. Honours: 1914/1915 Star.

Herbert Stanley **WARFIELD** (5 Sep 1891 - 26 Sep 1967), described as 5' 11 ¼" tall, fair complexion with brown eyes and fair hair, Roman Catholic (*QPF Recruit Register*). Born to John and Hannah, Drayton, Queensland. Sworn into the QPF on 1 Feb 1911, 19yrs 5mths, Reg no 1397, Roma Street Station, Brisbane (QSA AF3450). Enlisted with the AIF SERN

4269 on 27 Jun 1915. Embarked with the 15th Australian Infantry Battalion aboard HMAT *Kyarra A55* on 3 Jan 1916. Awarded Distinguished Conduct Medal on 3 Sept 1918, for conspicuous gallantry and devotion to duty while acting as platoon commander during an advance. Returned to Australia on 19 Jul 1919. Re-appointed to the QPF on 25 Sep 1919, Petrie Terrace Police Depot, Brisbane. Dismissed 8 Jan 1922 for assaulting a man at Mt Cuthbert (QSA AF3450). Died 26 Sep 1967, and buried in the Clifton Cemetery, Queensland. Honours: 1914/1915 Star; British War Medal; 1919 Victory medal; 1919 Distinguished Conduct Medal (Commonwealth of Australia Gazette, 4 Feb 1919, p. 124, position 10). Brother to: Sydney Warfield AIF and John Warfield AIF. Photographs: PM4564.

John WARFIELD (Oct 1893 - 28 Mar 1918 KIA), described as 5' 9 ½" tall, sallow complexion with blue eyes and brown hair, Roman Catholic (*QPF Recruit Register*). Born to John and Rose, Dulacca, Queensland. Sworn into the QPF on 11 Jan 1912, 18yrs 3mths, Reg no 1547, Maryborough Station, Brisbane (QSA AF3075). Enlisted in AIF SERN 4267 on 12 October 1915. Embarked with the 47th Australian Infantry Battalion aboard HMAT *Kyarra A55* on 3 Jan 1916. Wounded in France, sent to England and admitted to hospital on 6 Aug 1916. Sergeant Warfield was killed in action at Dernancourt, France on 28 Mar 1918. Honours: 1914/1915 Star; British War Medal; 1919 Victory medal. Brother to: Sydney Warfield AIF and Herbert Stanley Warfield AIF. Killed in action. Photographs: PM4558.

Sydney WARFIELD (Apr 1896 - 20 Feb 1945), described as 6' tall, sallow complexion with brown eyes and brown hair, Church of England (*QPF Recruit Register*). Born to John and Hannah, Drayton, Queensland. Sworn into the QPF on 22 Jun 1915, 19yrs 2mths, Reg no 2048, Petrie Terrace Police Depot, Brisbane (QSA AF3330). Enlisted with the

AIF SERN 4628 on 31 Aug 1915. Embarked with the 15th Australian Infantry Battalion aboard HMAT *Kyarra A55* on 3 Jan 1916. Returned to Australia on 6 Sep 1919. Re-appointed to the QPF on 8 Jan 1920, Reg no, Petrie Terrace Police Depot, Brisbane. Resigned on 19 Jul 1920 (QSA AF3330). Died 20 Feb 1945. Honours: 1914/1915 Star; British War Medal; 1919 Victory medal. Brother to Herbert Warfield AIF and John Warfield AIF.

John Henry WEDDERICK (19 Feb 1890 - 17 Dec 1934), described as 5' 9 ¾" tall, fair complexion with hazel eyes and brown hair, Church of England (*QPF Recruit Register*). Born to Hans and Annie, Toowoomba, Queensland. Sworn into the QPF on 10 Jul 1911, 21yrs 5mths, Reg no 1457, Roma Street Station, Brisbane (QSA AF3761). Enlisted with the AIF SERN 499 on 25 October 1915. Embarked with the 42nd Australian Infantry Battalion aboard HMAT *Borda A30* on 5 Jun 1916. Returned to Australia on 10 Mar 1918. Resumed duty with the QPF on 1 Jan 1919, Cairns Station. Retired on 1 Jan 1926 (QSA AF3761). Died 17 Dec 1934, and buried in plot M at Mareeba Pioneer Cemetery. Honours: British War Medal; Photographs: *The Queenslander Pictorial*, supplement to *The Queenslander*, 17 Jun 1916, p. 26 (SLQ Image No 702692-19160617-s0026-0041).

Harry WELLS (1885 - 31 Mar 1918 KIA), described as 5' 8 ¾" tall, fresh complexion with blue eyes and ginger hair, Church of England (*QPF Recruit Register*). Born to Mark and Martha, Kent, England (*Australia, Death Index, 1787-1985-* Reg no 9128). Five years in the Kent County Constabulary at Dartford and Swanby Stations (Ruge, 'Wells'). Sworn into QPF on 25 Mar 1914, 29yrs 2mths, Reg no 1840, Roma Street Station (QSA AF3264). Enlisted in AIF on 19 Apr 1915 SERN 440. Embarked with the 26 Infantry Battalion aboard HMAT *Ascanius A11* on 24 May 1915. Sergeant Wells wounded in abdomen at Pozieres, France on 28 Jul 1916, transferred to England, re-joined battalion 28 Dec 1916. Killed in action in Ploegsteert Wood, Belgium on 31 Mar 1918. Honours: 1914/1915 Star; British War Medal; 1919 Victory Medal; Photographs: *The Queenslander Pictorial*, supplement to *The Queenslander*, 05 Jun 1915, p. 26 (SLQ Image No 702692-19150605-s0026-0047). Killed in action.

Henry William 'Harry' WESTCOTT (28 Jun 1890 - 24 Feb 1938), described as 5' 9¾" tall, dark complexion with blue eyes and brown hair, Church of England (*QPF Recruit Register*). Born to William and Ann, Mackay, Queensland. Sworn into the QPF on 26 Apr 1912, 20yrs, Reg no 1602, Petrie Terrace Police Depot, Brisbane. Resigned on 22 Jan 1915 (QSA AF3613). Enlisted with the AIF SERN 10508 on 25 Sep 1915. Embarked with the 11th Australian Light Horse Regiment, Machine Gun Section aboard HMAT *Afric A19* on 05 Jan 1916. Returned to Australia on 14 Jan 1919. Married Mary Edith Hobbs on 16 Sep 1919. Re-appointed to the QPF on 22 Apr 1920, 28yrs, Reg no 2461, Petrie Terrace Police Depot, Brisbane. Resigned on 15 Dec 1923 (QSA AF3613). Died 24 Feb 1938, and buried in the Mackay City Cemetery. Honours: 1914/1915 Star; British War Medal; 1919 Victory medal.

Frederick Alexander WHITE (Jun 1883 - 10 Jun 1918 KIA) described as 5' 11" tall, dark complexion with brown eyes and dark hair, Presbyterian (*QPF Recruit Register*). Born in North Pine, Queensland, Australia. Sworn into the QPF on 30 Apr 1909, 25yrs, Reg no 1244, Roma Street Station, Brisbane (QSA AF3107). White joined the AIF on 07 Sep 1915, the 25th Battalion, SERN 4782. On 24 Nov 1916, White was wounded in action near Flers, receiving gunshot wounds to the right ankle. He returned to the front line in 1917 and was wounded again with shrapnel to the right shoulder on 20 Mar, near Vaux-Vraucourt. Following months of recovery, he returned to the front on 31 Jul 1917, but soon succumbed to 'trench fever' and had to be hospitalised in England for six months. White requested to return to active duty, re-joining his battalion in France on 25 Mar 1918. The 25th Battalion was involved in heavy fighting at Morlancourt on 10 Jun 1918. Frederick's half-brother Albert was with the same battalion, they were both killed in action on the same day. They are buried a short distance apart in Beacon Cemetery near Sailley-le-Sec (NAA 1847797). Honours: 1914/1915 Star; British War Medal; 1919 Victory medal. Photographs: PM4559.

Edgar WHITING (7 Jul 1878 - unknown), described as 5' 8" tall, sallow complexion with brown eyes and brown hair, Church of England (*QPF Recruit Register*). Born in Leystone, Essex, England. Served 12 years with the East Kent Regiment and seven years with the Royal Canadian Regiment. Sworn into the QPF on 8 Jul 1914, 35yrs, Reg no 1880, Roma Street Station, Brisbane (QSA AF3266). A British citizen appointed to the rank of Lieutenant with the AIF on 22 Feb 1915. The AIF record mentioned his previous military service in 'Swat Valley' North West India, 1897-8 (the First Mohmad campaign) and South Africa 1901-2 (the Second Boer War) (NAA 8386535). Embarked with the 25th Australian Infantry Battalion aboard HMAT *Aeneas A60* on 29 Jun 1916. Invalided to Australia suffering Rheumatism and flat feet on 3 Mar 1916. Discharged from the QPF on 17 Nov 1919 (QSA AF3266). Honours: 1914/1915 Star; British War Medal; 1919 Victory medal.

Fenwick Watson WILSON (11 Jun 1878 - 22 Jun 1919), described as 5' 10 ½" tall, fair complexion with blue eyes and fair hair, Church of England (*QPF Recruit Register*). Born to Henry and Emilee, Braidwood, New South Wales. Sworn into the QPF on 12 Mar 1908, 29yrs 9mths, Reg no 1120, Petrie Terrace Police Depot, Brisbane. Selected to take responsibility for escorting the horse 'Brisbane' to England to present it to his Majesty King George V as a coronation gift in July 1911 (QSA AF3070). Enlisted with the AIF SERN 1965 on 27 Oct 1915. Embarked with the 2nd Australian Remount Unit aboard HMAT *RMS Orontes* on 10 Nov 1915. Members of the Remount Service were often Boer War veterans, and expert horsemen who cared for and trained the horses acquired for use by the AIF. Returned to Australia on 22 Jan 1917, after having spent long periods in various hospitals in Egypt with pneumonia, bronchitis, Nile fever and lamblia intestinalis. Resumed duty with the QPF on 18 Jun 1917, Petrie Terrace Police Depot, Brisbane. Resigned on 28 Feb 1918 (QSA AF3070). Died 22 Jun 1919, and buried in Bermagui Cemetery, New South Wales. Honours: 1914/1915 Star; British War Medal; 1919 Victory medal; Photographs: PM4553.

Robert WRIGHT (31 Jul 1886 - 22 Apr 1960), described as 5' 9 ½" tall, fair complexion with blue eyes and fair hair, Presbyterian (*QPF Recruit Register*). Born to James and Helen, Durisdeer, Dumfriesshire, Scotland. Sworn into the QPF on 26 Apr 1912, 25yrs, Reg no 1603, Petrie Terrace Police Depot, Brisbane. Resigned 4 Nov 1915 (QSA AF2824). Enlisted with the AIF SERN 874 on 10 Nov 1915. Embarked with the 42nd Australian Battalion aboard HMAT *Borda* on 5 Jun 1916. Wounded in action on 24 Apr 1918 from gunshot wounds to the head and left ear. Married Margaret Strang Hill at Ayr, Scotland on 11 Jun 1919. Returned to Australia on 27 Feb 1920. Re-appointed to the QPF on 22 Mar 1920, Reg no 1603, 34yrs, Roma Street Station, Brisbane. Retired on 31 Jul 1946 (QSA AF2824). Died 22 Apr 1960. Honours: 1914/1915 Star; British War Medal; 1919 Victory medal.

1916

William Henry BEAVIS (22 Sep 1897 - 03 May 1942), described as 5' 10" tall, dark complexion with brown eyes and dark hair, Church of England (*QPF Recruit Register*). Born to Francis and Alice, Allora, Queensland (Australia Birth Index Reg No 002639). Sworn into the QPF on 8 Nov 1915, 18yrs 6mths, Reg No 2086, Roma Street Station, Brisbane. Dismissed from the QPF on 18 Oct 1916 (QSA AF2932). Enlisted with the AIF SERN 6939 on 27 Oct 1916. Embarked as SERN 7103 with the 15th Australian Infantry Battalion aboard HMAT *Beltana A72* on 25 Nov 1916. Court Marshalled for deserting on 6 Nov 1917 and sentenced to 10 years penal servitude. Court Marshall paperwork incorrect, re-joins battalion 2 Dec 1917 then ordered back to prison. In and out of hospital and military prison until 23 Jan 1918 when sentence commuted to two years. 18 Nov 1918 released from prison and remainder of sentence suspended. On 19 Nov 1918, re-joined 15th Battalion. Returned to Australia on 9 Aug 1919. Discharged from the AIF on 17 Sep 1919 (NAA 3064472). Died 3 May 1942, and buried in plot 1-63a-32 in the Lutwyche Cemetery, Brisbane (*Australia Cemetery Index, 1808-2007*). Honours: 1915 Star; British War Medal; 1919 Victory Medal.

John Michael BEIRNE (08 Sept 1887 - 26 Mar 1946), described as 5 '8 ¾" tall, fresh complexion with blue eyes and brown hair, Roman Catholic (*QPF Recruit Register*). Born to James and Ellen, Boyle, County Roscommon, Ireland. Served in the Royal Irish Constabulary, Belfast from 25 Oct 1907 until 9 Sep 1913. Sworn into the QPF on 11 Dec 1913, 26yrs 3mths, Reg No 1792, Roma Street Station, Brisbane. Dismissed from the QPF on 14 Feb 1916 (QSA AF2853). Enlisted with the AIF SERN 30082 on 22 Mar 1916. Embarked with the 3rd Australian Field Artillery Brigade aboard HMAT *Benalla A24* on 9 Nov 1916. Returned to Australia on 20 Oct 1919 (NAA 3070638). Discharged from the AIF on 15 Dec 1919. Died 26 Mar 1946 and buried in the Rookwood Cemetery, New South Wales. Honours: 1914/1915 Star; British War Medal; 1919 Victory Medal.

Clarence Herbert BLANDFORD (23 Jan 1893 - 09 Oct 1969), described as 5' 9" tall, sallow complexion with brown eyes and brown hair, Church of England (*QPF Recruit Register*). Born to Woodgate and Edith, Rockhampton, Queensland (Australia Birth Index 1788-1922, Reg no 011818, p. 2130). Sworn into the QPF on 22 Jun 1915, 22yrs, Reg no 2034, Roma Street Station, Brisbane. Resigned 16 Oct 1916 (QSA AF3603). Enlisted with the AIF SERN 631 on 26 Sep 1916. Embarked with the 12th Australian Machine Gun Company aboard HMAT *Ascanius A11* on 11 May 1917. Admitted to Belton Park Hospital, Grantham, England, on 11 Nov 1917, suffering from severe Pneumonia. 18 Aug 1918 admitted to Beaufort War Hospital, Bristol, England, suffering from tuberculosis and a bacterial infection. Returned to Australia on 25 Dec and discharged from the AIF on 26 Dec 1919 (AIF enlistment paperwork). Re-appointed to the QPF on 9 May 1921, 28yrs, Reg no 2533, Roma Street Station, Brisbane. Dismissed 7 Dec 1923. (*QPF Recruit Register*). Died 09 Oct 1969. Honours: 1914/1915 Star; 1919 British War Medal; 1919 Victory Medal.

Richard Joseph BODLEY (08 Jun 1880 - 18 Aug 1964), described as 6' tall, fresh complexion with blue eyes and fair hair, Roman Catholic

(*QPF Recruit Register*). Born to John and Mary, Dublin, Ireland (Ireland, Select Births and Baptisms, 1620-1911). Sworn into the QPF on 1 Jul 1908, 28yrs, Reg no 1151, Police Depot, Brisbane. Resigned 30 Nov 1908. Re-appointed to the QPF 15 Sep 1909, 29yrs, Reg no 1272, Police Depot, Brisbane (QSA AF3254). Enlisted with the AIF SERN 1432 on 5 Jan 1916. Embarked with the Australian Flying Corps aboard HMAT *Shropshire A9* on 11 May 1917. Returned to Australia 6 May 1919 and discharged from the AIF on 20 Jul 1919. Resigned from the QPF on 16 Oct 1919. Died 18 Aug 1964 and buried in a Brisbane cemetery. Honours: 1914/1915 Star; British War Medal; 1919 Victory Medal.

Robert BOWLES (09 Mar 1893 – 03 Oct 1958), described as 5' 8½" tall, dark complexion with brown hair and brown eyes, Congregational (*QPF Recruit Register*). Born to George and Ellen, Maryborough, Queensland (*UK, Commonwealth War Graves, 1914-1921 and 1939-1947* p. 36). Sworn into the QPF on 07 Jan 1916, 22yrs, Reg no 2135, Roma Street Station (QSA AF5857). Resigned 09 Oct 1916 to join the AIF. Embarked with the 4th Australian Pioneer Battalion aboard HMAT *Beltana A72* on 25 Nov 1916. While he sustained no battle wounds, was hospitalised twice with fever and written up for the loss of his kit. Returned to Australia 09 Mar 1919. Re-appointed to the QPF on 18 Jul 1919, Reg no 2411, Ipswich Station. Retired 09 Mar 1953 (QSA AF5857). Died on 03 Oct 1958 and buried in plot A-558 at the South Brisbane Cemetery, Brisbane. Honours: 1914/1915 Star; 1919 British War Medal; 1919 Victory Medal; Photographs: PM0442.

Edward James BRADFIELD (17 Sep 1891 - 17 Jul 1959), described as 5' 10½" tall, dark complexion with brown eyes and brown hair, Presbyterian (*QPF Recruit Register*). Born to Charles and Agnes, Allora, Queensland (*Australia Birth Index, 1788-1922*, Reg no 002999, p. 2557). Sworn into the QPF on 31 Mar 1915, 23yrs, Reg no 2003, Police Depot, Brisbane. Resigned 20 Sep 1916 (QSA AF5665). Enlisted with the AIF SERN 3315 on 25 Oct 1916. Embarked with 4th Australian Pioneer Battalion aboard HMAT *Beltana A72* on 25 Nov 1916. Returned to Australia on 1 Jul 1919. Re-appointed to the QPF on 16 Jan 1920, 28yrs, Reg no 2429, Roma Street station, Brisbane (*QPF Recruit Register*). Married Norah Margaret Cooke on 6 Jul 1921 (Ancestry). Retired 17 Sep 1951. Died 18 Jul 1959, and buried in plot 6-6-38 in the Lutwyche Cemetery, Brisbane. Honours: 1914/1915 Star; British War medal; 1919 Victory Medal.

Robert Thomas BROCK (Mar 1891 - unknown), described as 5' 8 ½" tall, dark complexion with blue eyes and brown hair, Roman Catholic (*QPF Recruit Register*). Born to William and Christina, Sydney, New South Wales. Sworn into the QPF on 28 Apr 1914, 23yrs 1mth, Reg no 1844, Stables, Petrie Terrace Police Depot (QP AF2777). Dismissed 9 Jun 1915. Enlisted with the AIF SERN 634 on 11 Oct 1916. Embarked 11 May 1917 with the 12 Machine Gun Company aboard HMAT *Ascanius A11* from Melbourne. Returned to Australia on 25 Apr 1918 (NAA3126250). Honours: 1914/1915 Star; 1919 British War Medal; 1919 Victory Medal; Photographs: *The Queenslander Pictorial,* supplement to *The Queenslander,* 18 Aug 1917, p. 23 (SLQ Image No 702692-19170818-s0023-0089).

Charles Henry BROOK (31 Mar 1887 - 06 Oct 1960), described as 5' 8 ½" tall, dark complexion with brown eyes and brown hair, Church of England (*QPF Recruit Register*). Born to John and Charity, Blantyre, Harrisville, Queensland. Served as Supernumerary Constable at Depot for three weeks but resigned on 5 May 1910. Sworn into the QPF on 23 May 1911, 24yrs 2mths, Reg no 1422, Mount Elliot Station, Queensland. Married Mabel Smith on 2 Sep 1915. Resigned from the QPF on 2 Feb 1916 (QSA AF2852). Enlisted with the AIF SERN 34652 on 11 May

1916. Embarked with the 5th Australian Field Artillery Brigade aboard HMAT *Suevic A29* on 21 Jun 1917. Returned to Australia on 5 Apr 1919 (NAA3128487). Died on 31 Mar 1960 (*Australia, Death Index, 1787-1985*, Reg no B060855, p. 317). Honours: 1914/1915 Star; 1919 British War Medal; 1919 Victory Medal.

William John BURNELL (Sep 1892 - 04 Aug 1918 KIA), described as 5' 9" tall, dark complexion with hazel eyes and dark hair, Roman Catholic (*QPF Recruit Register*). Born to Patrick and Mary, Ipswich, Queensland. Sworn into the QPF on 22 Dec 1914, 22yrs 3mths, Reg no 1960, South Brisbane Station, Brisbane. Resigned 20 Nov 1916 (QSA AF2921). Enlisted with the AIF SERN 37314 on 23 Nov 1916. Embarked with the 13th Australian Field Artillery Brigade aboard HMAT *Port Sydney A15* on 5 Nov 1917 (Enlistment paperwork). During 4/5th August 1918, batteries took up positions east of Amiens in anticipation of the advance planned for 8 Aug 1918. During this period Burnell was killed by enemy shellfire on 4 Aug 1918, in France and buried in plot 4-A-12 in the Longueau British Cemetery, Picardie, France (Commonwealth War Graves, 1914-1921 and 1939-1947). Honours: 1919 British War Medal; 1919 Victory Medal. Killed in action.

Kenneth CAMPBELL (1891 - unknown), described as, complexion with eyes and hair, (*QPF Recruit Register*). Born to ? and Margaret, Meeniyan, Victoria. Sworn into the QPF on 08 Nov 1912, 21yrs, Reg no 1575, South Brisbane Station, Brisbane (QSA AF4851). Enlisted with the AIF SERN 3044 on 31 Oct 1916. Embarked with the 41st Australian Infantry Battalion aboard HMAT *Wiltshire A18* on 07 Feb 1917. Returned to Australia on 04 Jul 1919. Re-appointed with the QPF on 16 Jan 1920, 26yrs, Roma Street Station, Brisbane. Dismissed 24 Sep 1932 (QSA AF4851). Honours: 1914/1915 Star; British War Medal and 1919 Victory Medal.

Charles Frederick COTT (03 Jun 1890 - Sep 1967), described as 5' 10" tall, dark complexion with hazel eyes and brown hair, Roman Catholic (*QPF Recruit Register*). Born to Edward and Elizabeth, St George, Queensland. Sworn into the QPF on 28 Apr 1914, 23yrs 9mths, Reg no 1847, Stables, Petrie Terrace Police Depot, Brisbane. Resigned 11 Dec 1916 (QSA AF4670). Enlisted with the AIF SERN 3295 on 11 Dec 1916. Embarked with the 5th Australian Light Horse Regiment aboard HMAT *Port Sydney A15* on 09 May 1917. Returned to Australia on 25 Apr 1919. Re-appointed to the QPF on 27 Jan 1920, 29yrs 6mths, Reg no 2433, Roma Street Station, Brisbane. Married Maud Isabel Hogan on 07 Jul 1920. Retired 13 Mar 1943 (QSA AF4670). Died Sep 1967 and buried in plot 11-26-25 at Toowong Cemetery, Brisbane. Honours: 1914/1915 Star; 1919 British War Medal; 1919 Victory Medal.

Timothy **COUGHLAN** (20 Oct 1884 - unknown), described as 5' 10" tall, dark complexion with blue eyes and brown hair, Roman Catholic (*QPF Recruit Register*). Born in Ireland. Served with the Royal Irish Constabulary 02 Apr 1907 - 24 Jul 1912. Sworn into the QPF on 06 Nov 1912, 28yrs, Reg no 1667, Roma Street Station, Brisbane (QSA AF4180). Enlisted with the AIF SERN 2397 on 27 Jul 1916. Embarked with the 48th Australian Infantry Battalion aboard HMAT *Anchises A68* on 28 Aug 1916. Returned to Australia on 17 Mar 1919. Resumed duty with the QPF on 10 Jul 1919, 34yrs, Petrie Terrace Police Depot, Brisbane. Retired 6 Sep 1934 (QSA AF4180). Honours: 1914/1915 Star; 1919 British War Medal; 1919 Victory Medal.

Cecil Reginald CUTTIFORD (Oct 1886 - 13 May 1958), described as 6'1¼" tall, fresh complexion with hazel eyes and fair hair, Church of England (*QPF Recruit Register*). Born in Dublin, Ireland. Three years with 2nd West Lancashire Infantry Volunteers. Sworn into the QPF on

01 Oct 1909, 23yrs, Reg no 1273, Petrie Terrace Police Depot, Brisbane. Resigned on 31 Dec 1911. Re-appointed on 25 Mar 1914, 27yrs, Reg no 1837, Roma Street Station, Brisbane (QSA AF4038). Married Helena Maude Williams on 23 Feb 1916 in Brisbane (Australian Marriage Index 1788-1950). Enlisted with the AIF SERN 6964 on 08 Jun 1916. Embarked with the 9th Australian Infantry Battalion aboard HMAT *Kyarra A55* on 17 Nov 1916. Returned to Australia on 30 Jan 1918 (Enlistment paperwork NAA 3481390). Resumed QPF duty on 22 Apr 1918, 32yrs, Reg no 1837, Water Police, Brisbane. Dismissed 23 Jan 1931 (QSA AF4038). Died 13 May 1958. Honours: 1914/1915 Star; British War Medal; 1919 Victory medal; Photographs: PM1975.

Llewellyn DADSWELL (04 Nov 1892 - 29 Dec 1944), described as 5' 8 ½" tall, dark complexion with brown eyes and dark brown hair, Church of England (*QPF Recruit Register*). Born to William and Catherine, Brighton, Sussex, England. Served six years with the A.S.C. (Army Service Corps) in England. Married Minnie Robertson in Oct 1911 in Brighton, England. Sworn into the QPF on 2 Jun 1915, 22yrs, Reg no 2020, Roma Street Station, Brisbane. Resigned on 06 Aug 1916 (QSA AF4289). Enlisted with the AIF on 07 Aug 1916 as part of the 11th Depot Battalion. Discharged 14 Nov 1916, at his own request (NAA 3482003). Re-appointed to the QPF on 01 May 1918, 25yrs, Reg no 2325, South Brisbane Station, Brisbane. Retired on 25 Jan 1936 (QSA AF4289). Died 29 Dec 1944 and buried in plot 4 at the Mackay City Cemetery.

John Henry DALY (12 Sep 1891 - unknown), described as 5' 11" tall, fresh complexion with blue eyes and fair hair, Church of England (*QPF Recruit Register*). Born to Richard and Helena, Ballydehob, Cork, Ireland. Sworn into the QPF on 07 Jan 1916, 24yrs 4mths, Reg no 2137, Roma Street Station, Brisbane (QSA AF4510). Enlisted with the AIF SERN 637 on 07

Aug 1916. Embarked with the 12th Australian Machine Gun Company aboard HMAT *Ascanius A11* on 11 May 1917. Returned to Australia on 04 Jan 1919 (NAA 3484947). Re-appointed to the QPF on 15 Jul 1919, 27yrs 10mths, Reg no 2504, Petrie Terrace Police Depot, Brisbane. Resigned 28 Aug 1919. Re-appointed 20 Nov 1920, 29yrs 3mths, Roma Street Station, Brisbane. Retired 27 Apr 1940 (QSA AF4510). Honours: 1914/1915 Star; British War Medal; 1919 Victory medal.

John DOCKERY (Jun 1887 - unknown), described as 5' 10" tall, fresh complexion with grey eyes and brown hair, Roman Catholic (*QPF Recruit Register*). Born to Stephen and Maria, Roscommon, Ireland. Sworn into the QPF on 10 Mar 1915, 27yrs 9mths, Reg no 1991, Petrie Terrace Police Depot Brisbane. Resigned 06 Mar 1916 (QSA AF2863). Enlisted with the AIF SERN 2935 on 18 Nov 1916. Embarked with the 41st Australian Infantry Battalion aboard HMAT *Demosthenes A64* on 23 Dec 1916. Returned to Australia on 09 February 1919. Discharged from the army 09 May 1919 (NAA 3510113). He moved back to Kilkenny, Ireland and died there, date unknown. Honours: 1914/1915 Star; British War Medal; 1919 Victory medal.

Michael EGAN (21 June 1886 - unknown), described as tall 5' 9¼", fresh complexion with blue eyes and brown hair, Roman Catholic (*QPF Recruit Register*). Born to ? and Mary, Ballydaly, King's County, Ireland. Sworn into the QPF on 30 Sep 1913, 27yrs 3mths, Reg no 1771, Petrie Terrace Police Depot, Brisbane. Resigned 04 Oct 1915 (QSA AF2810). Enlisted with the AIF SERN 1815 on 30 Mar 1916. Embarked with the 41st Australian Infantry Battalion aboard HMAT *Boorara A42* on 16 Aug 1916. Returned to Australia on 21 Dec 1917 and discharged, suffering from a Ventral Hernia, on 19 Mar 1918 (NAA 3536064). Honours: 1914/1915 Star; British War Medal; 1919 Victory medal.

Private William ELSDALE/ ELLSDALE/ ELISDALE (23 Dec 1886 – 1916 KIA) Billy Elsdale was the only Queensland Police tracker to volunteer in the First World War. He is also 'believed to be the first Aboriginal digger to die during action in France' ("*X*" – *The Life and Death of a Courageous Digger*, Queensland State Archives Blog, 1 Jul 2016). William 'Billy' Elsdale was born David Elsdale, also David Hibbit, on 23 December 1886 in Warra, Dalby, Queensland. His birth was registered on 18 February 1887, which likely led to Billy giving his birth year as 1887 in later documentation (David Elsdale, record no 850, *Births in District of Balonne in the Colony of Queensland, 1887*, 1887/C/85; Birth Certificate 000085, p. 4388; NAA B2455, Elsdale, B., First Australian Imperial Force Personnel Dossiers, 1914-1920). His birth certification indicates that his parents were not married. Billy's mother, Matilda 'Tilly' Hibbit/ Hibbitt (transcribed as Lilly), was Aboriginal. All evidence indicates she was related to the Aboriginal people with the surname Hibbit (or variations of), local to the area ('Public Curator form in Billy's intestacy file', QSA ID 1413637). She was born in 1864-65, to Catherine Orchard and Richard Hibbitt in Currawildi, Belmont/ Balonne Shire/ Maranoa, Queensland (cited differently across Tilly's vital records; Matilda Busiko died on 16 (17) Jan 1947; married William Busiko, (Reg 1891/C19; death registration 000769, p. 296), Mungallala, Maranoa Region, QLD). Billy's photograph was published in *The Queenslander Pictorial*, supplement to *The Queenslander*, 24 Jun 1916 (p. 27, SLQ Image No 702692-19160624-s0027-0010).

Billy's military service file described him as six feet and half an inch tall (184cm), 161 pounds (73kg), measuring 39 and a half inches (1m) circumference across the chest with brown eyes and black hair, complexion - 'half-cast'[sic] and his religion is listed as Roman Catholic. He signed his application with a cross, which indicates he could not write. Billy was one of the first few Aboriginal Australians to enlist with the Australian Imperial Forces, when World War I was declared on 28 June 1914 ("*X*" – *The Life and Death of a Courageous Digger*).

Billy's father was David Hugh Elsdale (10 May 1860 – 15 April 1938, Dalby) born in Warra, Queensland to British parents, who arrived in the Australian colonies from the United Kingdom (David Elsdale, Dalby Monumental Cemetery, Division: M, Section: Roman Catholic, Old, Plot: 3210; Memorial ID 210560907). David's mother, Anne Laird, was born in Belfast in 1826, and she arrived in New South Wales on the *James Moran* on 6 October 1841 ('Anne Laird 1841 October James Moran', *Assisted Immigrant Passenger Lists, 1828-1896* NSW). Per the passenger list, Anne was a nursemaid, a Roman Catholic, and could read. David's father, Alexander Hugh Elsdale, was born in 1818 in Lancaster, Lancashire. At 20 years of age, he was convicted of larceny (stealing a watch) at the Lancaster Quarter Sessions and sentenced to be transported for 10 years to New South Wales. Prior to his transportation, Alexander was detained in a prison hulk (a decommissioned ship used as a floating prison). According to the gaoler's notes in *Prison Hulk Registers and Letter Books, 1802-1849*, he was single, literate (could both read and write), a weaver with a previous conviction, and a 'very bad character' as well as an 'indifferent character' (*UK, Prison Hulk Registers and Letter Books, 1802-1849* for Alexr Elsdale *Justitia Register 1837-1844*). Having spent three months on the convict hulk, he departed England on 27 July 1838 on the *Earl Grey* along with another 289 convicts, arriving to New South Wales on 21 November 1838 (Microfilm Roll 90, Class and Piece Number HO11/11, Page Number 315 (159)).

In June 1843, Alexander was granted a ticket of leave, allowing him to stay in the district of Scone, NSW. Billy's grandfather went on to have a life that was not unusual for an ex-convict at the time, a life that saw a man end up on both sides of law enforcement (more on ex-convicts turn policemen see Dukova, *To Preserve and Protect: Policing Colonial Brisbane*, UQP 2020). On 2 January 1853, Alexander H Elsdale was awarded £2 from the Police Reward Fund Account, for 'activity and zeal in the apprehension of three prisoners who escaped from the watch-house Bargo' – he was an officer with the local police force ('Alexander H Elsdale', *Australia, Returns of the Colony, 1822-1857*, NSW). However, in 1855 he was charged with stealing from a dwelling house – but subsequently found not guilty (Alexr. Hugh Elsdale Clerk of the Peace Registers, *Registers of criminal cases tried at Goulburn, 1853-1859, Australia, Criminal Court Records, 1830-1945*, NSW). Then, on 7 April 1857, Alexander was dismissed from the Goulburn Police Force for neglect of duty ('District of Goulburn. Reports of Crime, Etc for Police Information No 24', April 14, 1857, *Police Gazette*, NSW, p. 2). Alexander Elsdale died on 21 March 1865 in Queensland, just before his son, David Hugh, Billy's father, turned five.

From 1913, until enlisting with the AIF on 10 September 1915, Billy worked as a police tracker at the Charleville Station, Queensland Police Force (*"X" – The Life and Death of a Courageous Digger*). Police trackers were not sworn officers and did not have legal authority. The roles police trackers performed differed from the Native Mounted Police paramilitary squads, in that the trackers worked alone or in pairs, and relied on their knowledge of the country to locate missing persons or recover property. In Queensland, the Native Mounted Police were disbanded at the turn of the twentieth century nearly a decade earlier, after operating from 1849 into the early years of the 20th century (see Jonathan Richards, *The Secret War: A True History of Queensland's Native Police*, UQP 2008; https://frontierconflict.org/).

Billy is mentioned in the Charleville file correspondence, where he is described as 'a good all around man and a fine horseman'. Notably, the police and military records, resignation from the force and enlistment with the AIF in Brisbane, are both dated 10 September 1915 (QP25629, Elsdale, QSA ITM317674). Out of nearly 200 men who left the Queensland Police Force to serve in the AIF, Billy was the only Aboriginal man.

John Maynard's study of the First World War records published in Joan Beaumont and Alison Cadzow's *Serving Our Country: Indigenous Australians, War, Defence, and Citizenship* reveals that the greatest numbers of Aboriginal men signed up in the years 1914 to 1916; '[o]f the 989 records of Aboriginal men examined, 641 of them had enlisted before 1917 (the latest research places the number at over 1,000, IndigenousHistories.com, Apr 23 2021; *Aboriginal Enlistment During World War I - This Month in History*, ANU). However, it is important to note that in contrast to other states, there was a spike in Queensland enlistment in 1917 (Maynard, 'The First World War', in Joan Beaumont and Alison Cadzow, *Serving Our Country: Indigenous Australians, War, Defence, and Citizenship*. UNSWP, 2018, p. 66). In May 1917, under the pressures of the war, the military regulations were altered to allow the enlistment of 'half-castes' provided that 'one of the parents is white and of European origin' (Siobhan McDonell & Mick Dodson, 'Race, Citizenship and Military Service', in *Serving Our Country*, p. 41). Before 1917, it was left to the medical officer to decide on the suitability of the candidate.

In 1901, the Australian Constitution declared all Australians, including Indigenous people, to be British subjects. Despite this overarching status, in practice the rights afforded to Indigenous people were negotiated through legislative arrangements between various states and the Commonwealth (McDonell & Dodson, p. 35). The colonial (later state) governments adopted numerous and conflicting definitions of 'Aboriginality', sometimes excluding 'half-caste' people from specific provisions and at other times including them. Blood-quantum distinction - an individual's racial category - was viewed as being based on their genealogy, so a 'half-caste' Aboriginal person was also categorised as European.

Private Billy Elsdale, whose 'complexion' was described as 'half-cast' [sic], was initially assigned to the 9th Infantry Battalion. He embarked on the HMAT *Wandilla* in Brisbane on 31 January 1916. On 3 March 1916, Elsdale arrived in Alexandria, Egypt, and soon after on 23 April 1916, he was transferred to the newly formed 47th Battalion, in Serapeum. On 2 June, the unit sailed on the SS *Caledonia* to France joining the British Expeditionary Forces. Arriving in Marseilles on 9 June, the battalion was later stationed at Outtersteen, near the Belgian border. On 7 July 1916, just four weeks later, Billy Elsdale was killed in action during operations at Fleurbaix ("Advertising" *Townsville Daily Bulletin* 12 October 1916; Death certificate 543097, QLD BDM) he is interred at the Rue-David Military Cemetery, Fleurbaix along with 87 other Australian servicemen (Plot II. E. 44, memorial ID 56182661Fleurbaix, Departement du Pas-de-Calais, Nord-Pas-de-Calais, France).

In *Battle Scarred*, Craig Deayton describes the conditions the 47th Battalion faced, where the trenches were 'not dug into the ground due to the high-water table, but 'were instead raised sandbag breastworks' (Craig Deayton, *Battle Scarred*, Big Sky Publishing, 2011, p. 47. Special thanks to Tim Lycett for this reference). Deayton writes:

Over time, enemy artillery fire had caused gaps in the breastworks and their snipers concentrated on these gaps waiting for passing soldiers who weren't taking enough care to conceal themselves. Elsdale was one of those and he was picked off by a sniper while passing one of these gaps. He was the first soldier of the 47th Battalion to be killed in action.

Australian War Memorial records indicate that the 47th Battalion was formed in Egypt on 24 February 1916 as part of the 'doubling' of the AIF. Approximately half of its new recruits were Gallipoli veterans from the 15th Battalion, and the other half, fresh reinforcements from Australia. Reflecting the composition of the 15th, the new battalion was composed mostly of men recruited in Queensland and Tasmania. The new battalion was incorporated into the 12th Brigade of the Australian Division. Arriving in France on 9 June 1916, the 47th entered the trenches of the Western Front for the first time on 3 July ('47th Australian Infantry Battalion', *Australian War Memorial*).

Maynard recounts the battles and the men that succumbed to wounds and diseases in the trenches. He concludes, 'these casualties indicate, Aboriginal men took part in some of the fiercest fighting on the Western Front, a theatre where the individual soldier was almost eclipsed by artillery and other weapons of industrialised war' (Maynard, p. 71).

Following Billy's death, his personal belongings were released to Jack Cockrane, his designated next of kin: 'disc, purse, 3 coins, aluminium ring, crucifix, photo, military certificates' (NAA B2455, Elsdale, B., p. 59). The to and fro in the departmental correspondence reveals that Jack was also an Aboriginal man and had been employed by Cobb and Co for 25 years. Jack was 'located through press' as earlier attempts to find him were unsuccessful. This in part could be because he was illiterate (NAA B2455, Elsdale, B., p. 53). Billy's parents are not featured in the departmental correspondence until 1923, when his father David Hugh Elsdale responded in writing to the department's request to receive Billy's war medals (Victory Medal and the British War Medal, NAA B2455, Elsdale, B).

Terence Joseph GANZER (1 Mar 1895 - 26 Apr 1976), described as 5' 8" tall, fresh complexion with blue eyes and brown hair, Roman Catholic (*QPF Recruit Register*). Born to Christopher and Ellen, Murphy's Creek, Queensland. Sworn into the QPF on 08 Aug 1916, 21yrs 5mths, Reg no 2194, Petrie Terrace Police Depot, Brisbane (QSA AF3659). Enlisted with the AIF SERN 3114 on 17 Nov 1916. Embarked with the 5th Light Horse Regiment aboard HMAT *Hymettus A1* on 03 Feb 1917. Returned to Australia on 29 Jun 1919. Re-joined the QPF on 25 Sep 1919, 24yrs 6mths, Petrie Terrace Police Depot, Brisbane. Married Evelyn Violet Walton on 14 May 1924 in Charleville, Queensland. Resigned 30 Jun 1924 (QSA AF3659). Died 26 Apr 1976. Honours: 1914/1915 Star; British War Medal; 1919 Victory medal.

John HERBERT (8 Nov 1888 - 09 Sep 1918 KIA), described as 5' 11" tall, dark complexion with hazel eyes and light brown hair, Roman Catholic (*QPF Recruit Register*). Born to George and Ellen, Maryborough, Queensland. Sworn into the QPF on 14 Feb 1908, 19yrs 4mths, Reg No 1099, Woolloongabba Station (QSA AF3131). Enlisted in the AIF on 02 October 1916. Embarked with the 31st Australian Infantry Battalion aboard HMAT *Wiltshire A18* on 07 Feb 1917. Wounded by shrapnel to the back and thorax at the Somme, France on 07 Sep 1918. Died of his wounds on 09 Sep 1918. Buried in the Heath Cemetery, Harbonnieres, Picardie, France. Honours: 1914/1915 Star; British War Medal; 1919 Victory medal. Killed in action. Photographs: PM4565.

William Robert HOLZNAGEL (01 Aug 1894 - 03 Jul 1959), described as 5' 8" tall, fair complexion with hazel eyes and fair hair, Lutheran (*QPF Recruit Register*). Born to Ferdinand and Johanna, Gatton, Queensland. Sworn into the QPF on 22 Jun 1915, 20yrs 10mths, Reg no 2910, Petrie Terrace Police Depot Stables, Brisbane. Resigned 20 Jun 1916 (QSA AF2904). Enlisted with the AIF SERN 2910 on 13 Sep 1916. Embarked with the 47th Australian Infantry Battalion aboard HMAT *Marathon A74* on 27 Oct 1916. Returned to Australia on 13 Jul 1919 (NAA 5822982). Died 03 Jul 1959. Honours: 08 Apr 1918 Recommended for the Military Medal; 1914/1915 Star; British War Medal; 1919 Victory medal; Photographs: *The Queenslander Pictorial*, supplement to *The Queenslander*, 30 Jun 1917, p. 24 (SLQ Image No 702692-19170630-s0024-0067).

Thomas HOWARD (1 Dec 1891- 11 Apr 1948), described as 6' 1 ¾" tall, dark complexion with brown eyes and brown hair, Roman Catholic (*QPF Recruit Register*). Born to James and Mary, Ballybaughan, County Clare, Ireland. Sworn into the QPF on 11 Feb 1914, 22yrs 2mths, Reg no 1809, Roma Street Station, Brisbane. Resigned 13 May 1916 (QSA AF2901). Enlisted with the AIF SERN 7266 on 29 May 1916. Embarked with the 9th Australian Infantry Battalion aboard HMAT *Ayrshire A33* on 24 Jan 1917. Returned to Australia on 3 Mar 1919. Continued in Army Service until 1924 when he went into private business. Died 11 Apr 1948 in Granville, New South Wales. Honours: 07 Oct 1918: Military Medal (Imperial) (*London Gazette*, p. 11840/pos63); 1914/1915 Star; British War Medal; 1919 Victory medal.

Joseph IMHOFF (30 Jun 1886 - 09 Jun 1953) described as 5' 9" tall, dark complexion with blue eyes and brown hair, Presbyterian (*QPF Recruit Register*). Born to Phillip and Caroline, Spring Creek, Queensland (*Australia, Birth Index, 1788-1922*; Reg no 002168). Sworn into the QPF on 26 Apr 1912, 25yrs, Reg no 1584, Roma Street Station, resigned 8

Jul 1914 (QSA AF2638). Enlisted with the AIF on 2 May 1916 SERN 394. Embarked with the 7th Machine Gun Company on 19 Sep 1916 aboard the HMAT *Commonwealth A73*. Recommended for Meritorious Service Medal on 24 Sep 1918. Returned to Australia on 8 Sep 1919 (NAA 7366045). Re-sworn into the QPF on 1 Dec 1920, 34yrs, Reg no 2509, Fortitude Valley Station, retired 30 Jun 1946 (QSA AF2638). Married Edith Biggs on 7 Jun 1922. Died 9 Jun 1953 and buried in the Mt Thompson Memorial Gardens and Crematorium. Honours: 1914/1915 Star; British War Medal; 1919 Victory medal; 1919 Military Medal.

William Joseph LAWSON (Dec 1891 - unknown), described as 5' 8" tall, fresh complexion with brown eyes and brown hair, Church of England (*QPF Recruit Register*). Born to ? and Francis, Liverpool, England. Served three years in the Territorials. Sworn into the QPF on 30 Sep 1913, 21yrs 11mths, Reg no 1780, Petrie Terrace Police Depot, Brisbane. Resigned on 20 Mar 1916 (QSA AF2877). Enlisted with the AIF SERN 7 on 23 Mar 1916. Embarked with the 11th Australian Machine Gun Company aboard HMAT *Borda A30* on 05 Jun 1916. Returned to Australia on 21 Jun 1919 (NAA 7377958). Honours: 1914/1915 Star; British War Medal; 1919 Victory medal.

Frank LEWIS (13 Oct 1892 - 1 Mar 1967), described as 5' 8 ½" tall, fair complexion with blue eyes and fair hair, Church of England (*QPF Recruit Register*). Born to Oswald and Louisa, Georgetown. Queensland. Sworn into the QPF on 10 Mar 1915, 22yrs 5mths, Reg no 1993, Petrie Terrace Police Depot, Brisbane. Resigned 23 Aug 1916 (QSA AF4443). Enlisted with the AIF SERN 7261 on 23 Nov 1916. Embarked with the 8th Australian Infantry Battalion aboard HMAT *Ballarat A70* on 19 Feb 1917. Returned to Australia on 30 Jan 1918. Re-appointed to the QPF on 07 Mar 1919, Reg no 2386, 26yrs, Petrie Terrace Police Depot, Brisbane.

Retired on 04 Dec 1938 (QSA AF4443). Died 01 Mar 1967 and buried in plot ANZAC-1-E-306 in the Mount Gravatt Cemetery and Crematorium, Brisbane. Honours: 1914/1915 Star; British War Medal; 1919 Victory medal.

John Reynette LEWIS (12 Jul 1890 – 04 Aug 1972), described as 5' 10 ½" tall, reddish complexion with blue eyes and brown hair, Church of England (*QPF Recruit Register*). Born to Elizabeth Jane and ? in Kings County, Ireland. Served for five years with 'Military Police, Ireland (NAA 8203546). Sworn into the QPF on 10 Mar 1915, 24yrs 8mths, Reg no 1994, Fortitude Valley (QSA AF3990). Enlisted with the AIF on 26 Jul 1916 SERN 6570. Embarked with the 26th Infantry Battalion aboard HMAT *Wiltshire A18* on 7 Feb 1917. Returned to Australia on 05 Nov 1917. Re-appointed to the QPF on 15 Feb 1918, 27yrs, Reg no 2314, Gladstone Station. Suffered from tuberculosis and unfit to continue working, retired 16 Mar 1930 (QSA AF3990). Died 04 Aug 1972, and buried in Woronora Memorial Park, New South Wales. Honours: 1914/1915 Star; British War Medal; 1919 Victory medal.

Robert LOW (23 Nov 1888 - 26 Mar 1962), described as 6' 2" tall, ruddy complexion with hazel eyes and auburn hair, Roman Catholic (*QPF Recruit Register*). Born to Robert and Annie, Brewarrina, New South Wales. Sworn into the QPF on 01 Feb 1913, 24yrs 2mths, Reg no 1704, Roma Street Station, Brisbane. Resigned 23 Dec 1915 (QSA AF4052). Enlisted with the AIF SERN 6008 on 25 Oct 1916. Embarked with the Tunnelling Companies aboard HMAT *Ulysses A38* on 25 Oct 1916. Returned to Australia on 09 Oct 1919. Re-appointed to the QPF on 01 Jul 1920, 31yrs, Petrie Terrace Police Depot, Brisbane. Retired on 16 Nov 1931 (QSA AF4052). Died 26 Mar 1962. Honours: 1914/1915 Star; British War Medal; 1919 Victory medal.

George MARSH (11 Jul 1897 - 23 Apr 1947), described as 5' 10" tall, fair complexion with blue eyes and fair hair, Church of England (*QPF Recruit Register*). Born to George and Mary, Gayndah, Queensland (*Australia Birth Index, 1788-1922*; Reg no 1282). Sworn into the QPF on 21 Dec 1915, 18yrs, Reg no 2116, Gladstone Station, resigned 30 Sep 1916 (QSA AF2925). Enlisted with the AIF SERN 3136 on 04 Oct 1916. Embarked with the 4th Pioneer Battalion aboard the HMAT *Kyarra A55* on 17 Nov 1916. Returned to Australia on 06 Nov 1918. Re-appointed to the QPF on 03 Mar 1919, 20yrs, Reg no 2385, Roma Street Station. Married Winifred Dorothy Smithers on 15 May 1920 in Brisbane. Died of tuberculosis on 23 Apr 1947 at Kalinga, Brisbane (QSA AF2925). Honours: 1914/1915 Star; British War Medal; 1919 Victory medal.

Francis Henry McIVER (31 Oct 1881 - 06 Nov 1940), described as 5' 11", fresh complexion with hazel eyes and brown hair, Roman Catholic (*QPF Recruit Register*). Born to Patrick and Mary, Sandon, Victoria. Sworn into the QPF on 01 Nov 1910, 29yrs, Reg no. 1378, Criminal Investigation Branch, Brisbane (QSA AF4569). Married Mary Ellen Luby at Brisbane on 04 Nov 1913. Made available to Commonwealth for Defence duty in connection with the AIF in Cairo and England between 14 Mar 1916 and 12 Feb 1917. Died 06 Nov 1940 at Lister Hospital, Townsville from acute streptococcal appendicitis.

Vincent William O'BRIEN (04 Aug 1893 - 06 Jul 1966), described as 5' 8 ½" tall, fair complexion with hazel eyes and brown hair, Roman Catholic (*QPF Recruit Register*). Born to Felix and Bridget, Toowong, Brisbane. Sworn into the QPF on 17 Aug 1914, 21yrs, Reg no 1902, Petrie Terrace Police Depot, Brisbane. Dismissed 24 Dec 1915 (QSA AF2841). Enlisted with the AIF SERN 1965 on 19 Jan 1916. Embarked with the 49th Australian Infantry Battalion aboard HMAT *Clan McGillivray A46* on 01 May 1916. Suffered a severe gunshot wound to right thigh in France on 20 April 1918 and was invalided to the United Kingdom. Re-joined 41st Battalion on 18 Sep 1918. Returned to Australia on 20 May 1919. Died 06 Jul 1966 and buried in plot 7A-476 at the Nudgee Cemetery, Brisbane. Honours: 1914/1915 Star; British War Medal; 1919 Victory medal.

David Hubert 'Hugh' O'DONOGHUE (26 Jun 1893 - 20 Jun 1918 KIA), described as 5' 9½" tall, pale complexion with brown eyes and brown hair, Roman Catholic (*QPF Recruit Register*). Born to Edward and Mary, Clonmel, Tipperary, Ireland (AIF Attestation Papers, NAA 7991842). Sworn into the QPF on 31 Mar 1915, 31yrs 9mths, Reg No 2009, Maryborough Station (QSA AF3153). Enlisted with the AIF on 20 Apr 1916 SERN 6076, indicating prior experience with AIF infantry and the military police (AIF Attestation Papers). Embarked with the 9th Battalion aboard *Itonus A50* on 08 Aug 1916. Shot in the chest and fractured a femur, died 20 Jun 1918, at a French dressing station shortly after being admitted. Buried in Hazebrouck Cemetery, Nord, Nord-Pas-de-Calais, France. Honours: 1914/1915 Star; British War Medal; 1919 Victory medal. Killed in action.

Edgar STEPHENSON (Sep 1888 - 26 Jun 1955), described as 5' 11" tall, sallow complexion with blue eyes and brown hair, Church of England (*QPF Recruit Register*). Born to Arthur and Annie, Concord, New South Wales. Sworn into the QPF on 22 Dec 1914, 26yrs 3mths, Reg no 1971, Roma Street Station, Brisbane. Resigned 20 Mar 1916 (QSA AF2871). Enlisted with the AIF SERN 3122 on 24 Apr 1916. Embarked with the 2nd Australian Light Horse Regiment aboard HMAT *Hymettus A1* on 03 Feb 1917. Suffered tachycardia and debility on route to Egypt and was returned to Australia on 11 Jul 1917, and medically discharged on 29 Sep 1917 (NAA 8089396). Died 26 Jun 1955, and buried in the Mount Thompson

Memorial Gardens and Crematorium, Holland Park West, Brisbane City. Honours: 1914/1915 Star; British War Medal; 1919 Victory medal.

William John STERNE (29 Apr 1879 - 09 Sep 1963), described as 5' 9¼" tall, fair complexion with blue eyes and fair hair, Presbyterian (*QPF Recruit Register*). Born to Johannes and Louise, Warwick, Queensland. Sworn into the QPF on 6 Dec 1900, 21yrs 8mths, Reg no 413, Petrie Terrace Police Depot, Brisbane. Resigned (QSA AF4298). Enlisted with the AIF SERN 5116 on 22 Mar 1916. Embarked with the 31st Australian Infantry Battalion aboard HMAT *Hororata A20* on 14 June 1917. Wounded in action on 4 Jul 1918, a gunshot wound to the thigh and a compact fracture of the femur. Invalided home to Australia on 6 May 1919. Re-appointed to the QPF on 27 Jan 1921, 41yrs 11mths, Reg no 647, Petrie Terrace Police Depot, Brisbane. Married Neta May Smallwood 26 Apr 1927. Retired on 22 Jan 1936 (QSA AF4298). Died on 09 Sep 1963. Honours: 1914/1915 Star; British War Medal; 1919 Victory medal.

Robert William STYNES (20 Jul 1889 - 05 Jun 1960), described as 5' 10 ¼" tall, fair complexion with blue eyes and fair hair, Church of England (*QPF Recruit Register*). Born to Robert and Mary, Murtoa, Victoria. Sworn into the QPF on 10 Aug 1912, 23yrs, Reg no 1643, Petrie Terrace Police Depot, Brisbane. Resigned 17 Oct 1914 (QSA AF2678). Enlisted with the AIF SERN 323 on 10 Feb 1916. Embarked with the 3rd Australian Pioneer Battalion aboard HMAT *Wandilla A62* on 06 Jun 1916. Received gunshot wound to the left shoulder on 06 Apr 1918 and received a severe gunshot wound to the abdomen on 22 Aug 1918. Returned to Australia on 04 Mar 1919 (NAA 8095801). Died 05 Jun 1960, and buried in a Victorian Cemetery. Honours: 1914/1915 Star; British War Medal; 1918 Military Medal (*Commonwealth of Australia Gazette*, 27 Nov 1918, p. 2264, position 66); 1919 Victory medal.

Edward Daniel TOOHEY (14 Nov 1888 - 26 Aug 1960), described as 6' tall, ruddy complexion with hazel eyes and brown hair, Roman Catholic (*QPF Recruit Register*). Born to Daniel and Julie, Murchison, Victoria. Sworn into the QPF on 02 Jul 1912, 23yrs 7mths, Reg no 1624, Petrie Terrace Police Depot, Brisbane. Resigned 19 May 1916 (QSA AF2891). Enlisted with the AIF SERN 520 on 20 Jun 1916. Embarked with the 7th Australian Machine Gun Company aboard HMAT *Medic A7* on 16 Dec 1916. Returned to Australia on 13 Jul 1919 and discharged from the AIF on 31 Jan 1920 (NAA 8392215). Died 26 Aug 1960 and buried in Tatura Cemetery, Victoria. Honours: 1914/1915 Star; British War Medal; 1919 Victory medal.

Richard Blake TREAHY (14 Feb 1889 - 28 Oct 1959), described as 5' 9 ¾" tall, dark complexion with brown eyes and brown hair, Roman Catholic (*QPF Recruit Register*). Born to Thomas and Mary, Shepparton, Victoria. Sworn into the QPF on 1 Feb 1911, 22yrs, Reg no 1396, Petrie Terrace Police Depot, Brisbane. Resigned 1 Feb 1914 (QSA AF2566). Enlisted with the AIF SERN 6822 on 17 Feb 1916. Embarked with the 5th Infantry Battalion aboard HMAT *Ulysses A38* on 25 Oct 1916. Returned to Australia on 18 Jan 1919. Died 28 Oct 1959, and buried in plot LL7-1-3 at Melbourne General Cemetery, Melbourne, Victoria. Honours: 1911 Medal for Merit; 1914/1915 Star; British War Medal; 1919 Victory medal.

Thomas WALKER (04 May 1887 - 01 Jul 1942), described as 5' 8 ½" tall, fresh complexion with blue eyes and light brown hair, Church of England (*QPF Recruit Register*). Born in Bedford, England. Between 1910 – 1911 member of the Metropolitan Police (London). Immigrated to Canada. Member of the Royal North-West Canadian Mounted Police between 1911- 1915 (service details are from the QPF staff file, self-reported). Sworn into the QPF on 02 Aug 1915, 28yrs 3mths, Reg no 2068, Roma

Street Station, Brisbane. Resigned 14 Aug 1916 (QSA AF2934). Enlisted with AIF 19 Aug 1916 SERN 7792 and embarked with the 9th Battalion from Sydney on HMAT *A14 Euripides* on 31 Oct 1917. He returned to Australia on 28 Aug 1919. Joined New Guinea Police Force on 12 Sep 1924. As as police officer in Rabaul, he was taken prisoner by the Japanese during WW2. Walker died alongside other 1,053 POWs, when the Japanese POW ship *Montevideo Maru* was sunk by the American submarine, USS *Sturgeon* on 01 July 1942, off Luzon, Philippines.

William WRIGHT (20 Mar 1892 - unknown), described as 5' 8 ¼" tall, fair complexion with blue eyes and fair hair, Weslyan (*QPF Recruit Register*). Born in Derby, Derbyshire, England. Sworn into the QPF on 26 Nov 1912, 20yrs 8mths, Reg no 1695, Petrie Terrace Police Depot, Brisbane (QSA AF3416). Enlisted with the AIF SERN 2178 on 10 Apr 1916. Embarked with the 42nd Australian Infantry Battalion aboard HMAT *Clan McGillivray A46* on 07 Sep 1916. On 31 Jul 1917, East of Messines, William was mainly responsible for the rapid evacuation of the wounded in his sector. His courage and devotion to duty during the whole operation were of a very high nature. Returned to Australia on 25 Mar 1919. Resumed duty with the QPF on 17 Jul 1919, Petrie Terrace Police Depot, Brisbane. Dismissed on 25 Aug 1921 (QSA AF3416). Honours: 1915 Police Medal for Merit; 1914/1915 Star; British War Medal; 1917 Military Medal (*London Gazette* 28 Sept 1917, p. 10039, position 22); 1919 Victory medal.

1917

Frank Hawthorne BATE (20 Apr 1890 - 26 Jan 1977), described as 5' 9 ¼" tall, dark complexion with hazel eyes and brown hair, Church of England (*QPF Recruit Register*). Born to Forrester and Elizabeth, Brisbane, Queensland (NAA 3056129). Sworn into the QPF on 04 Jul 1913, 23yrs 2mths, Reg no 1731, South Brisbane Station (QSA AF4658). Enlisted with the AIF SERN 4436 on 11 Dec 1917. Embarked with the 11th Australian Light Horse Regiment aboard SS *Port Darwin* on 30 Apr 1918. Returned to Australia on 20 Jul 1919 (NAA 3056129). Re-sworn into the QPF on 02 Oct 1919, Reg no 1731, Roma Street Station (QSA AF4658). Married Margaret Katherine Burke on 14 Jan 1928 (deceased 18 Mar 1930). Married Clara Wilamina Albrecht on 01 Feb 1936. Retired 10 Jan 1943. Died 26 Jan 1977, buried in Eden Gardens Memorial Park, Warwick. Honours: 1914/1915 Star; 1919 British War Medal; 1919 Victory Medal.

Mervyn Thomas Stephen CAVANAGH (22 Feb 1894 - 24 Jun 1949), described as 5' 10" tall, fresh complexion with brown eyes and brown hair, Roman Catholic (*QPF Recruit Register*). Born to John and Jane, Warialda, New South Wales. Sworn into the QPF on 03 Oct 1916, 22yrs 7mths, Reg no 2212, Petrie Terrace Police Depot. Resigned 30 Jun 1917 (QSA AF3013). Enlisted with the AIF SERN 16404 on 02 Jul 1917. Embarked with the Australian Army Service Corps aboard HMAT *Borda A30* on 17 Jul 1918. Returned to Australia on 13 Jul 1919 (NAA 3221820). Died 24

Jun 1949, and buried in plot M2-15-3770 in the Rookwood Cemetery, New South Wales. Honours: 1914/1915 Star; British War Medal; 1919 Victory Medal. Photographs: PM4549.

John FORDE (Aug 1889 - unknown), described as 5' 8 ¼" tall, fresh complexion with grey eyes and brown hair, Roman Catholic (*QPF Recruit Register*). Born to John and ?, Corondolla, Ireland. Sworn into the QPF on 03 Nov 1914, 25yrs 3mths, Reg no 1947, Sandgate Station, Brisbane. Dismissed on 31 May 1917 (QSA AF3005). Enlisted with the AIF SERN 5271 on 20 Dec 1917. Embarked with the 31st Australian Infantry Battalion aboard SS *Ormonde* on 02 Mar 1918. Returned to Australia on 22 Nov 1919 and discharged from the army on 15 Feb 1920 suffering form bronchitis (NAA 4019140). Honours: 1914/1915 Star; British War Medal; 1919 Victory medal.

Marshall HARROD (Jul 1882 - unknown), described as 5' 9" tall, fresh complexion with blue eyes and brown hair, Church of England (*QPF Recruit Register*). Born to Robert and Sarah, Kirton, Lancashire, England. Sworn into the QPF on 02 Aug 1915, 33yrs 1mth, Reg no 2057, Fortitude Valley Station, Brisbane. Resigned 31 Jul 1916 (QSA AF2909). Enlisted with the AIF SERN 18092 on 16 Jan 1917. Embarked with the Australian Army Medical Corps aboard HMAT *Port Sydney A15* on 05 Nov 1917. Returned to Australia on 23 July 1919. Honours: 1914/1915 Star; British War Medal; 1919 Victory medal.

Squire JENNINGS (28 Aug 1883 - 23 Dec 1941), described as 5' 10" tall, sallow complexion with hazel eyes and brown hair, Church of England (*QPF Recruit Register*). Born to William and Nancy, Wakefield, West Yorkshire, England. Sworn into the QPF on 26 Nov 1911, 27yrs 11mths, Reg no 1469, South Brisbane Station, Brisbane. Resigned 14 Dec 1916 (QSA

AF2946). Enlisted with the AIF SERN 7075 on 17 Sep 1917. Embarked with the 25th Australian Infantry Battalion aboard SS *Canberra* on 16 Nov 1917. Returned to Australia on 12 Dec 1918 (NAA 7361572). Died 23 Dec 1941 and buried in a Brisbane cemetery. Honours: 1914/1915 Star; British War Medal; 1919 Victory medal. Photographs: *The Queenslander Pictorial*, supplement to *The Queenslander*, 15 Dec 1917, p 27 (SLQ Image No 702692-19171215-s0026-0009).

John William JINKINS (06 Oct 1890 - unknown), described as 5' 8 ½" tall, ruddy complexion with blue eyes and ginger hair, Roman Catholic (*QPF Recruit Register*). Born in Brisbane, Queensland. Sworn into the QPF on 04 Jul 1913, 22yrs 9mths, Reg no 1743, Landsborough Station, Queensland. Resigned in 1916 (QSA AF3113). Enlisted with the AIF on 06 Feb 1917. Spent 235 days at AIF Enoggera Camp and discharged from the army after he shot himself in the foot just prior to time he was supposed to board train for Sydney with his unit. Re-appointed to the QPF on 28 Sep 1917, Landsborough Station, Queensland. Resigned 23 August 1918 (QSA AF3113).

Herbert James McPHERSON (28 Jul 1889 - 4 Jul 1971), described as 5' 8 ½" tall, dark complexion with brown eyes and black hair, Presbyterian (*QPF Recruit Register*). Born to Charles and Sarah, Clydesdale, Victoria. Sworn into the QPF on 08 Nov 1915, 26yrs 3mths, Reg no 2102, Roma Street Station, Brisbane (QSA AF3106). Enlisted with the AIF SERN 20301 on 29 June 1917 at Brisbane. Resigned from the QPF on 31 Jul 1918. Married to Maud Dunning McLeod. Discharged medically unfit from the AIF suffering from chronic rheumatism on 09 Sep 1918. Died 4 Jul 1971 and buried in plot 3-24 at Albany Creek Memorial Park Cemetery, Bridgeman Downs, Brisbane.

Martin MULROONEY (May 1890 - unknown), described as 5' 8" tall, dark complexion with brown eyes and black hair, Roman Catholic (*QPF Recruit Register*). Born in Hertford, Ireland. Sworn into the QPF on 28 Apr 1914, 24yrs 2mths, Reg no 1856, Roma Street Station, Brisbane. Resigned 13 Oct 1917 (QSA AF3029). Enlisted with the AIF SERN 2453 on 17 Oct 1917. Embarked with the 11th Australian Light Horse Regiment aboard HMAT *Ulysses A38* on 19 Dec 1917. Returned to Australia on 03 Sept 1919 (NAA 7987637). Honours: 1914/1915 Star; British War Medal; 1919 Victory medal; Photographs: *The Queenslander Pictorial, supplement to The Queenslander,* 19 Jan 1918 p. 26 (SLQ Image No 702692-19180119-s0026-0039).

Michael ROACHE (24 Jun 1891 - 24 Aug 1918), described as 5' 10 ½" tall, dark complexion with brown eyes and brown hair, Roman Catholic (*QPF Recruit Register*). Born to Michael and Mary, Lillimur, Victoria. Sworn into the QPF on 03 Nov 1914, 23yrs 4mths, Reg no 1954, Petrie Terrace Police Depot, Brisbane. Resigned 29 Apr 1917 (QSA AF2996). Enlisted with the AIF SERN 7769 on 03 May 1917. Embarked with the 9th Australian Infantry Battalion aboard HMAT Euripides *A14* on 31 Oct 1917. He then proceeded with the 9th Battalion to France on 20 Aug 1918. Was wounded by shellfire three days later, on the 23 Aug and died of wounds the following day, 24 Aug 1918. He was buried in an isolated grave just west of Chuignolles, France but the exact location was lost, and he is now remembered on the Australian National Memorial at Villers-Bretonneux, France. Honours: 1914/1915 Star; British War Medal; 1919 Victory medal. Photographs: PM4556. Killed on active service.

Peter James 'Jim' STORMONTH (23 Apr 1884 - 24 May 1927), described as 5' 8 ¼" tall, fresh complexion with grey eyes and brown hair, Church of England (*QPF Recruit Register*). Born to Peter and Rachel,

Blaina, Monmouthshire, Wales. Joined the Imperial Army in 1903. Sworn into the QPF on 26 Jul 1911, 27yrs 3mths, Reg no 1475, Petrie Terrace Police Depot Stables, Brisbane. Resigned? (QSA AF3841). Enlisted with the AIF SERN Q20312 on 07 Jul 1917. Transferred to the Rifle Range Camp at Enoggera as part of the F.A. Reinforcements. Discharged 03 Apr 1918, at his own request for family reasons. Re-appointed to the QPF on 23 Oct 1919, Petrie Terrace Police Depot, Brisbane. Died 24 May 1927, from illness while on sick leave (QSA AF3841). Buried in section 15 of the Balmoral Cemetery. Honours: 1914/1915 Star; British War Medal; 1919 Victory medal.

John Paterson TAYLOR (23 Jun 1877 - 21 Nov 1918 KIA), described as 6' ¾" tall, fresh complexion with blue eyes and brown hair, Methodist (*QPF Recruit Register*). Born to John and Mary, Glebe, Sydney, New South Wales. Married Caroline Vera Coronel on 16 Oct 1907. Sworn into the QPF on 05 Feb 1909, 32yrs, Reg no 1202, New Farm Station, Brisbane; transferred to Water Police in 1911 where he injured his back lifting a boat (QS AF3154; Ruge 'Taylor'). Enlisted in the AIF SERN 14921 on 17 Feb 1917. Taylor initially joined the Australian Field Artillery in February 1917, but he re-injured his back on arrival in England. He then embarked with the 38th Australian Army Service Corps Company as a driver instead. Died on 21 Nov 1918, in Egypt from dysentery at the 87th General Hospital in Alexandria, and buried in the Hadra War Memorial Cemetery, Alexandria, Egypt. Honours: 1914/1915 Star; British War Medal. Killed on active service. Photographs: PM4566.

Thomas Josiah TAYLOR (8 Oct 1890 - 4 Aug 1968), described as 5' 9 ½" tall, sallow complexion with hazel eyes and brown hair, Church of England (*QPF Recruit Register*). Born to Joseph and Amy, Glencoe, New South Wales. Sworn into the QPF on 15 Feb 1915, Reg no 1988, 24yrs

4mths, Petrie Terrace Police Depot, Brisbane. Dismissed 27 Jul 1916 (QSA AF2919). Enlisted with the AIF SERN 6848 on 27 Apr 1917. Embarked with the 26th Australian Infantry Battalion aboard HMAT *Hororata A20* on 14 Jun 1917. Returned to Australia on 26 Oct 1917. Embarked with the 26th Australian Infantry Battalion aboard SS *Ormonde* on 02 Mar 1918. Returned to Australia on 10 Apr 1919, suffering from the mumps. Died 04 Aug 1968, and buried in the Glen Innes Cemetery, New South Wales. Honours: 1914/1915 Star; British War Medal; 1919 Victory medal. Photographs: *The Queenslander Pictorial*, supplement to *The Queenslander*, 23 Jun 1917, p. 24 (SLQ Image No 702692-19170623-s0024-0011).

1918

Robert Stewart CHRISTIE (23 Feb 1882 - 18 Mar 1945), described as 5' 8 ¼" tall, fresh complexion with blue eyes and brown hair, Presbyterian (*QPF Recruit Register*). Born to Charles and Margaret, St Vigeans, Arbroath, Forfarshire, Scotland. Spent 3 years in the South African constabulary under Colonel Baden Powell. Sworn into the QPF on 26 Jul 1911, 29yrs, Reg No 1461, Roma Street Station, Brisbane. Married Elizabeth Mulvenna on 21 Jan 1913, without consent of the Commissioner and was required to resign but allowed to return because of his good work. Resigned and reappointed on 08 Apr 1914 (QSA AF4551). Enlisted with the AIF SERN 58076 on 18 Jul 1918. Embarked with the 9th Australian Infantry Battalion aboard HMAT *Bakara A41* on 04 Sep 1918. Returned to Australia on 28 Aug 1919. Reappointed to the QPF on 06 Nov 1919, 32yrs, Reg No 1841, Roma Street Station, Brisbane. Retired 20 Feb 1941 (QSA AF4551). Died on 18 Mar 1945, and buried in plot 8-344 at the Balmoral Cemetery, Brisbane. Honours: South African medal (5 clasps); 1913 Queensland Police Medal for Merit; 1914/1915 Star; 1919 British War Medal; 1919 Victory Medal; Photographs: PM4554.

John Alexander CLARK (12 Nov 1889 - unknown), described as 6' tall, fair complexion with blue eyes and fair hair, Presbyterian (*QPF Recruit Register*). Born to Alfred and Ellen, Peterhead, Aberdeenshire, Scotland. Served two years with Gordon Highlanders (Territorials), Scotland. Sworn into the QPF on 02 Aug 1915, 25yrs 9mths, Reg No 2052, Roma Street Station, Brisbane. Resigned 23 Oct 1918 (QSA AF3134). Enlisted with the AIF on 28 Oct 1918. Nil Embarkation due to Armistice signing. Discharged from the AIF 31 Dec 1918.

Laurence O'BRIEN (9 Jan 1894 - 14 May 1941), described as 6' 1 ½" tall, dark complexion with hazel eyes and brown hair, Roman Catholic (*QPF Recruit Register*). Born to David and Julia, Warwick, Queensland. Sworn into the QPF on 06 Nov 1912, 19yrs 10mths, Reg no 1675, Petrie Terrace Police Depot, Brisbane (QSA AF3711). Enlisted with the AIF SERN 53309 on 06 Mar 1918. Embarked with the 1 to 8 (Queensland) Reinforcements aboard RMS *Osterley* on 08 May 1918. Returned to Australia on 23 Jul 1919. Re-appointed to the QPF on 23 Oct 1919, Petrie Terrace Police Depot, Brisbane. Resigned on 24 Jan 1925 (QSA AF3711). Honours: 1914/1915 Star; British War Medal; 1919 Victory medal.

David SINCLAIR (16 Jun 1892 - unknown), described as 5' 10 ½" tall, dark complexion with hazel eyes and brown hair, Presbyterian (*QPF Recruit Register*). Born in Halkirk, Scotland. Sworn into the QPF on 11 Apr 1916, 22yrs 11mths, Reg no 2169, Roma Street Station, Brisbane. Resigned 01 Oct 1918 (QSA AF3514). Enlisted with the AIF SERN Q24530 on 06 Oct 1918, discharged on 19 Dec 1918, 'due to the termination of his period of enlistment' (NAA 8084687). Re-appointed to the QPF on 12 Dec 1918, Brisbane. Dismissed from police service on 30 Dec 1922 (QSA AF3514).

William WATSON (7 Dec 1887 - 28 May 1936), described as 5' 11½" tall, ruddy complexion with hazel eyes and brown hair, Presbyterian (*QPF Recruit Register*). Born in Dumfriesshire, Scotland. Sworn into the QPF on 26 Apr 1912, 24yrs, Reg no 1601, Petrie Terrace Police Depot, Brisbane.

Married Eva Kathleen Fullerton on 18 Feb 1913, without the consent of the Commissioner of Police. Required to resign on 30 June 1914 but reappointed same day (QSA AF4213). Enlisted with the AIF SERN 58206 on 18 May 1918. Embarked with the 1 to 8 (QLD) Reinforcements aboard HMAT *Bakara A41* on 04 Sep 1918. Returned to Australia on 19 Apr 1919. Resumed duty with the QPF on, Reg no 1875, Charters Towers, Queensland. Retired on 09 Feb 1935 (QSA AF). Died on 28 May. Honours: 1914/1915 Star; British War Medal; 1919 Victory medal; Photographs: *The Queenslander Pictorial,* supplement to *The Queenslander,* 26 Jan 1918, p. 26 (SLQ Image No 702692-19180126-s0026-0066).

Appendix A
Queensland Police Force Lists

Members of the Police Force who have enlisted for active service with the Australian Imperial Forces up to 31st Dec 1916, QPM, p. 1.

APPENDIX A   141

```
Ach.Sgt. A.A. Bock                    J.F. Ruhle
Const.  W. Peters                     W.H. Hartwig
        T.J. Judge                    J.R. Bodley
        J.F.J. Thompson Killed in action 23/7/16   W.J. Stone
        A. Cruickshank                G. Wright
        M.E. Matthews                 J. Birmingham
        F.W.J. Spencer                G. Burke
        D.J. Dodds                    C.R. Guthford
        T. Dedman  missing 28.5.16    J.H. Daly
        D. MacDonald                  T. Lewis
        J. McGillycuddy               G. Marsh
        O.H. Goodrich                 L. Dadswell
        J.C. Morris                   M. Harrod
        C.E. Castree                  E.J. Bradfield
        W.F. Bishop Killed in action 5/9/16   J.R. Lewis
        S. Adermann                   L. Johnson
        H.F. Shepherd                 F.J. Taylor
        F. Geise                      W.J. Burnell
        F.A. White                    P. Walker
        D. O'Donoghue (serving in Australia)   A.McLeod returned & resumed Police Duty 15/2/17
        S. Warfield                   J. Herbert
        A.C. Peters                   R. Bowle
        W.J. Nichol                   C.H. Hansford
        J. Kissane                    K. Campbell
        W.H. Player                   P.J. Ganzer
        H. Warfield                   G.C. Brodie
        J. Nichol                     F.C. Cott
        J.H. Douglas                  J.B. Singleton
        M. Bergin
        E.M. Riley
        J. Warfield
        W. Dumbrel
        J.H. Wedderich
        F. Melzer
        A.J. Curvey
        J. Fitzgerald
```

Members of the Police Force who have enlisted for active service with the Australian Imperial Forces up to 31st Dec 1916, QPM, p. 2.

1268 M (9)

LIST OF MEN WHO RESIGNED TO GO TO THE FRONT.

Names of Men who Resigned.		Names of Men who have Rejoined.	Names of Men who have claimed & received back services.
Brennan, T.V.	2699 AF		
Birmingham, P.(?)	2886 AF		
Bradfield, E.J.	2429 F	Bradfield, E.J. ✓	
Burwell, W.J.	2921 AF		
Bowles, R.	2411 F	Bowles, R. ✓	
Blandford, C.H.	2431 AF		
Brodie, G.O.	2428 F	Brodie, G.O. ✓	
Campbell, K.	2430 F	Campbell, K. ✓	
Cott, F.C.	2433 F	Cott, F.C. ✓	
Dadswell, L.	2325 F	Dadswell, L. ✓	
Harred, M.	2909 AF		
Johnson, E.	2918 AF		
Lucas, A.	2671 AF		
Lewis, F.	1993 F	Lewis, F.	Lewis, F.
Lewis, J.R.	1994 F	Lewis, J.R. ✓	Lewis, J.R.
McKee, P.H.	2688 AF		
Marsh, G.	2116 F	Marsh, G. ✓	Marsh, G.
Smith, G.	2697 AF		
Stynes, R.	2678 AF		
Singleton, J.C.	2947 AF		
Taylor, T.J.	2919 AF		
Walsh, E.	2664 AF		
Wright, W.E.	1095 F	Wright, W.E. ✓	Wright, W.E.
Walker, T.	2934 AF		
O'Connor, M.	3086 AF		
Vowles, P.	2666 AF		
A.J. Logan	2374 F	A.J. Logan	

9 FEB 1920

List of men who resigned to go to the front, 9 Feb 1920, QPM.

APPENDIX A

LIST OF OFFICERS, POLICE DEPARTMENT, WHO HAVE SERVED WITH
BRITISH EXPEDITIONARY FORCES, OR AUSTRALIAN IMPERIAL FORCES

NAME	RANK	FORCE SERVED WITH	REMARKS
Maddock J.E.M.	Clerk Head Office	A. I. F.	Returned & resumed duty.
Anderson S.	Constable	Imp. Army Reserv- 1st.	
Back O. McG.	"	"	
Casey T. J. J.	"	"	
Coughlan T.	"	"	
Hannigan J.	"	"	Returned & resumed duty.
Hembrey T. H.	"	"	
McLean M.	"	"	Killed in act.
Pastorelli E.H.	"	"	
Stormouth J.	"	"	
Adermann S.	Constable	A. I. F.	Returned & resumed duty. Since resigned.
Bell H.	"	"	
Bradley J. H.	"	"	
Bailey A. E.	"	"	
Bourke D. G.	"	"	Died of wound
Bock A. A.	Act. Sergt	"	Returned & resumed duty.
Bodley H. J.	"	"	
Bishop G. A.	Constable	"	Killed in Act
M. Bergin M.	"	"	
Burke J.	"	"	
Bate F. H.	"	"	
Connor F.	"	"	
Cloherty F.	"	"	Returned & resumed duty. Since resigned. Returned & since resumed do.
Cummins W. G.	"	"	
Campbell D. A.	"	"	Killed in act
Christiansen J.	"	"	
Cole B. G.	"	"	
Castree O. E.	"	"	Died of wound
Christie M. D.	"	"	
Corvey A. J.	"	"	
Cuttiford O. R.	"	"	Returned & resumed duty do.
Cruickshank A.	"	"	
Deshurst Geo.	"	"	Killed in Act do.
Devine P.	"	"	
Dodds D. J.	"	"	
Dedman T.	"	"	Killed in Ac
Douglas S. H.	"	"	
Dumbrell .	"	"	Killed in Ac
Daly J. H.	"	"	
Fitzgerald J.	"	"	
Gorman M. J.	"	"	Returned & resumed duty Since resign Died of woun
Graham J.	"	"	
Gilty A. A.	"	"	
Goodrich O. H.	"	"	Killed in Ac
Geles F. J.	"	"	
Genzer T. J.	"	"	

List of officers, Police Department, who have service with the British Expeditionary Forces, or Australian Imperial Forces, QPM, p. 1.

Name	Rank	Force Served With	Remark
Hartill H. J.	Constable	A.I.F.	
Hackney H.	"	"	
Harte M. E.	"	"	Returned and resumed duty
Hadland H. S.	"	"	
Hamilton H. J.	"	"	
Hartwig W. B.	"	"	
Herbert J.	"	"	
Johnston J.	"	"	Killed in Action
Judge T. J.	"	"	
Jinkins J. W.	"	"	Did not go to Resumed duty Since resigned
Kenny W. H.	"	"	
Kiddell W.	"	"	Returned and resumed duty. do.
King O.	"	"	
Kerr P.	"	"	
Kissane J.	"	"	
Lang A.	"	"	
Leader W. J.	"	"	
McLeod A.	"	"	Returned and resumed duty.
McLean C.I.	"	"	
Moynihan F.J.	"	"	Killed in Action
McKay W. A.	"	"	
Mulvey P.	"	"	Killed in Action
McDonald A.	"	"	
McAnbridge A.	"	"	
Morohan F. J.	"	"	
Matthews W. H.	"	"	Returned and resumed duty.
McDonald B.	"	"	
McGillycuddy T.	"	"	
Morris J. C.	"	"	
McPherson H. J.	"	"	Enlisted but did not go to front owing to injuries received. Resigned Killed in action
Nugent E.	"	"	
Nichol W.C.	"	"	
Nichol J.	"	"	
O'Loughlin T. C.	"	"	Returned. Discharged by Police Medical Board. Returned and resumed duty.
O'Brien W.	"	"	
O'Donoghue D.	"	"	
O'Brien L.	"	"	
Phelps M.N.R.	"	"	
Peters W.	"	"	
Peters A.	"	"	
Player W. B.	"	"	Returned and resigned. Did not resume duty. Died. Returned and resumed duty.
Ritchie R. D.	"	"	
Riley E.M.	"	"	
Ruhle J. F.	"	"	
Sutherland B. W.	"	"	
Smith S. J.	"	"	
Shepherd E. A.	"	"	
Spencer F. N. J.	"	"	
Shepherd H. F.	"	"	
Sterne W. J.	"	"	
Thompson J. S. V.	"	"	Died.
Taylor J. P.	"	"	
Vowles F.	"	"	Killed in Action
Whiting E.	"	"	
Welle H.	"	"	

List of officers, Police Department, who have service with the British Expeditionary Forces, or Australian Imperial Forces, QPM, p. 2.

APPENDIX A 145

List of officers, Police Department, who have service with the British Expeditionary Forces, or Australian Imperial Forces, QPM, p. 3.

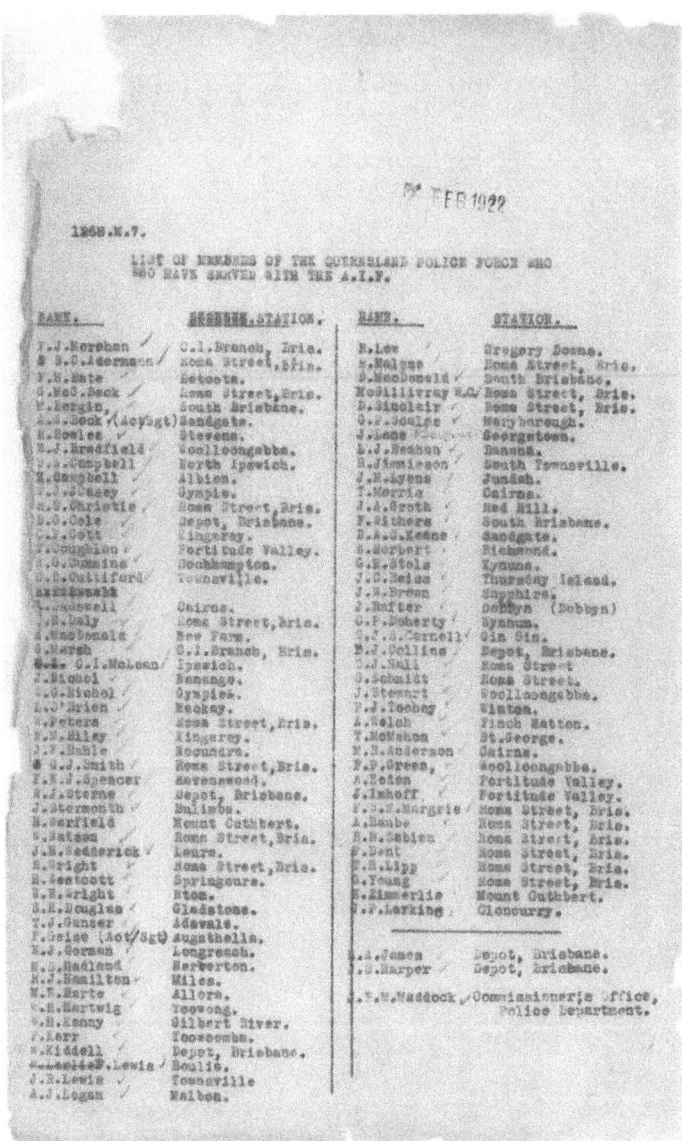

List of members of the Queensland Police Force who have served with the A.I.F., 7 Feb 1922, QPM.

Other publications

A History of the Dublin Metropolitan Police and Its Colonial Legacy

To Preserve and Protect: Policing Colonial Brisbane

www.ingramcontent.com/pod-product-compliance
Lightning Source LLC
Chambersburg PA
CBHW060157050426
42446CB00013B/2867